IN THE NAME OF GOD

Entrepreneurship as done by

Ali Khosravani

The Founder of
Auto Khosravani and Auto shenas

Written by:
Dr. Reza Yadegari
Dr. Mahshid Sanaeefard
The Winners of the Prestigious
Jalal Al-e Ahmad Literary Award
and
Aryaan Yadegari
Lilyaan Yadegari
The Second Generation Authors of the
Great Iranian Entrepreneur Book Collection

Kidsocado Publishing House
Vancouver, Canada

Phone: +1 (833) 633 8654
WhatsApp: +1 (236) 333 7248
Email: info@kidsocado.com
https://kidsocadopublishinghouse.com
https:/kidsocado.com

Serial Number: P2446190211
Title: Entrepreneurship as done by Ali Khosravani
Series Name: Iranian Great Entrepreneurs
Authors: Dr. Reza Yadegari, Dr. Mahshid Sanaeefard
Contributor Authors: Aryaan Yadegari, Lilyaan Yadegari
Copyist: Great Entrepreneur
ISBN: 978-1-77892-188-9
Metadata: Entrepreneurship/ Biography /Business & Economics
Book: Paperback
Pages: 106
Canada Publish Date: June 2024
Publisher: Kidsocado Publishing House

All Rights Reserved, including the right of production
in whole or part in any form.
Copyrigh@2024 by
Kidsocado Publishing House

- Introduction — 3
- The Greenlight — 5
- The life and world of Ali Khosravani — 7
- The analysis of the founder of Auto Khosravani and Auto Shenas — 67

Introduction

The work of identifying the greatest Iranian entrepreneurs got underway back in 1997 with the help and assistance of my wife Dr. Mahshid Sanaeefard, the Manager of the Great Iranian Entrepreneurs Publication. An exceptionally long and arduous task, which has enabled us to gain substantial insight into the world of entrepreneurship and job creation, and thus make history for the future generation of Iranians by helping found and chart a whole new path towards true success in business and industry alike.

Next to winning numerous international awards on this incredible journey of countless ups and downs, we have cooperated and collaborated extensively with some of Iran's highly accredited and most reputable higher learning centers, like Sharif Industrial University, University of Science and Technology, Alzahra University and Shahid Beheshti University. Moreover, we have also successfully established and registered the International Qualification and Certification Auditors Company or IQCA in Canada, whose main role and responsibility is to publish the life history of the greatest Iranian entrepreneurs to make them known by name to the other people in the world. IQCA has also been highly active in setting up and establishing an award presentation scheme in Iran in order to identify and introduce the country's most creative individuals and organizations, and thereby aid and assist with promoting them on a global scale.

It is hoped that as a special and leading group, we are able to introduce the most powerful Iranian women and me to the rest of the world and at the same time, identify and retell the life stories of the best role models for Iran's next generation.

Dr. Reza Yadegari
www.IBDC.ws

The Greenlight

The movement to transfer the experiences of the world's greatest entrepreneurs is one of the most important factors in helping the American and European companies and organizations' progress and improvement. These companies and organizations had concluded rather smartly that if a society wishes significant advancement and development, it must keep its eye on the experiences of the previous generation and not allow the young to incur costs on the system by experiencing and learning through trial and error. In line with the same notion, entrepreneurship has the potential to create notable transformation throughout a given society's various levels provided it is implemented using principles and plans that take advantage of the experiences of the proficient and skilled members. Allowing the young to take over across the world is certainly a commendable measure, which has also been taken in our beloved Iran as well, except that here the experiences of the previous generation of entrepreneurs and managers has never been made properly available for application by the new generation – something that has regrettably inflicted irrecoverable costs onto the country because of the continuous repetition of the same old mistakes. Our project to identify the greatest Iranian entrepreneurs, so that we may research their lives to understand the reasons and factors for their success started off back in 1997 simultaneously as the arrival of the novel science of entrepreneurship in Iran. Admittedly, the path has been a long one involving strenuous effort. In the years following the events of the Iranian Revolution, literary no entrepreneur in the country was willing to unveil and reveal herself or himself and the experiences she or he possessed.

In spite of this, we were quite determined to fulfil our goal of teaching and training the future generation by documenting and publishing the life stories and experiences of Iran's greatest entrepreneurs through a one-thousand-volume book aptly titled 'Entrepreneurship as done by …' What is presented in the book collection, is rare and valuable roadmap designed based on the experiences and performances of Iran's greatest economic minds, which undoubtedly can be a wonderful asset in guiding and directing anyone who intends to get involved in any type of commercial, production and service provision activity. We hope that our collection book can help open up doors and pave the way for Iran's new generation of young entrepreneurs, and also remain a lasting piece of literary work to remember us by.

Dr. Reza Yadegari
Dr. Mahshid Sanaeefard
Tehran, Iran 2024

The life and world of Ali Khosravani
Biography of Ali Khosravani

Childhood

I, Ali Khosravani, was born on September 12, 1978, in the Gisha neighborhood of Tehran. I was the firstborn in my family. I have one sister and two younger brothers. Hussein, my second brother, is 6 years younger than me and currently my best colleague in the automotive industry. My other brother, Reza, is approximately 20 years younger than me, born on May 23, 1997.

The Tale of Reza

Reza, who won a gold medal in the literary Olympiad, has a life quite different from mine and my other brother's. His journey is truly fascinating: When Reza was a child, his teachers expelled him from school, deeming him to have a slow processing mind and recommending enrollment in a school for mentally disabled children. This news greatly upset our mother, who found it hard to accept. Eventually, she agreed to send him to a special needs school. However, just a few days before Reza was scheduled to start there, I consulted a friend named Mr. "Jafari," who was the principal of another school. I asked him to enroll Reza in his school and allow him to remain there until the end of the academic year as an exception.

After Mr. Jafari asked me about the reason for referring Reza to the special needs school, I replied: "It seems like he doesn't pay any attention to the teacher's instructions in class and doesn't respond to any class questions or assignments." According to his teacher's statements, "He only sits quietly in class for the first ten minutes, then he wants to leave and can't stay calm in one place."

Mr. Jafari, who previously worked at SAMPAD ("SAMPAD" is an abbreviation for the National Organization for Development of Exceptional Talents, established in 1977 with the aim of monitoring the academic affairs of talented and intellectually gifted students in Iran.), said: "Bring Reza to me."

After seeing Reza, Mr. Jafari said to the relevant teacher: "I will register this student in my school, but you don't have to worry about him, and consider him a sort of independent listener. Don't be too strict with him if he wants to leave the class at any time, and try not to ask him too many questions." This way, we managed to enroll Reza in a regular school.

After a year passed, Mr. Jafari announced that he wanted to register Reza's name for the entrance exam of the gifted schools (Sampad schools). At first, we thought Mr. Jafari had made this decision to boost our morale and show kindness to Reza, as during those days, all families were trying to enroll their children in the entrance exams for gifted schools. I remember our family didn't even know the exact date of the entrance exam for gifted schools and its conditions. It's worth mentioning that every year, more than 90,000 students participate in this exam to try their luck in studying at these schools. With Mr. Jafari's insistence, my father finally accompanied Reza on the day of the exam, and Reza succeeded in achieving the seventh national rank in the gifted schools that year.

Our family only realized later that Reza was gifted, but because he had attention deficit hyperactivity disorder (ADHD), he struggled with attention and hyperactivity issues. He would grasp the lesson quickly at the beginning, but then lose interest, which made it difficult for him to pay attention to the teacher. As a result, his previous teachers thought he had a slow mind and behaved unusually.

Later on, Reza studied two majors simultaneously and managed to pursue sociology at the University of Tehran without taking the entrance exam. Currently, he has been accepted for PHD studies at a university in Germany to continue his education.

Mr. Sohrab

My mother used to be a school health teacher, but after giving birth to her first three children, who were born close in age, she resigned from her job and became a homemaker.

My father, Mr. Sohrab, was the longtime head of Iran Road Construction Company in Khuzestan. The company had constructed numerous roads in the Khorasan province. Even the Tehran-Qom highway, from Tehran to Hassanabad-Fashafouyeh, was built during my father's tenure, and the project management was taken over by the Kison Company from Fashafouyeh onwards.

My father initially was as a workshop manager at the construction company. Later, he owned a mosaic factory and for several years served as the head of the Union of Mosaic and Cement Factory Workers in Iran. Since 1972, alongside his factory, he also managed a car exhibition.

The atmosphere I opened my eyes to and grew up in, was filled with cars and the hustle and bustle of automobiles. When I reached adolescence and could step into the world of adults, my father officially became a businessman, dedicating himself to the car sales profession.

Throughout my school years, in the afternoons and after school hours, I would go to my father's place of business, and I even did my homework at the exhibition desk.

To me, my father was more like a mentor, and I often referred to him as "Mr. Sohrab" rather than "dad." Most of the time, relatives and elders would scold me, asking, "Why do you call your father Mr. Sohrab?" In response, I would say, "He's my boss all day at work, so when I'm at his workplace, I call him Mr. Sohrab. We only spend a quarter of the day together at home, so he feels more like Mr. Sohrab to me than dad."

From childhood, whenever people asked me, "What do you want to be when you grow up?" I would say, "Car salesman." I remember during middle school when the guidance teacher asked us to choose a role and play it in the career theater, I played the role of a businessman and car salesman. It might surprise you, but contrary to the environment I grew up in, I'm not particularly interested in cars and their options. For example, when I go to the hair salon, if there are several car magazines along with other family, cooking, and social magazines on the table, I always pick up the family magazine first and read it, then the car magazine.

I'm more interested in the car selling process than the models and types of cars. I'm not so passionate about cars that I have to ride the latest and most up-to-date model under any circumstances.

The exciting part of the car selling process for me is that when someone comes to the exhibition, I can guide them well to make their desired choice and leave satisfied with their purchase.

In the final year of high school, my father didn't allow me to attend the exhibition. Until then, my mother had been following up on our study and educational matters, and we thought Mr. Sohrab didn't even know what grade his children were in school.

My grades were good, and I was always among the top students in school. I remember only once, in the tenth grade, in a new math class, I failed an exam in the first semester. The school principal sent a letter home requesting one of my parents to come to school for follow-up. That day, Mr. Sohrab came to school and adamantly wanted to take me out from the school and not allow me to continue my education. Now, the principal and the math teacher started pleading with him, asking him to reconsider his decision.

In the presence of the teachers, Mr. Sohrab said to me, "Son, have I ever forced you to study?" I replied, "No." He asked, "Have I ever told you that you must study and become a doctor?" Again, I said, "No." He then said, "If you want to study, this is not the way. If you don't want to study, leave school right now, and I'll set up a shop for you. If you want to work, I'll provide you with all the resources. But if you want to study, the path you've chosen is not right, and I can't leave you to your own devices."

That was the first and last time I faced rejection during my schooling. My father always said, "Whatever you do, you must do it to the best of your ability. Even if you become a simple office worker, work so well and decently that when they need to downsize, you're the last option they consider."

Therefore, in my final year, my father didn't allow me to work at the car exhibition. He said, "You have exams, sit at home and study properly."

I remember that at that time, the university entrance exam was held in two stages, and the Azad University exam was also held on the 12th of Mordad. The day after the exam, exactly on the 13th of Mordad, 76, I returned to the car exhibition with Mr. Sohrab.

My father had a strong belief in hierarchy. I remember when I wanted to start working seriously, he allowed me to collaborate from the lowest level. I started with cleaning, then became a water carrier and a motorcycle courier, and after a few years, I became a delivery manager and office manager. Because I was very interested in this work, I endured all the hardships.

That same year, I was accepted into the Civil Engineering department at Azad University of Tehran. I wasn't particularly interested in civil engineering, but because it was a popular field and had become quite prestigious in those years, I enrolled in this major at Azad University.

During university, the head of our department, Mr. Vakili, always told me, "You neither do your job properly nor study well. Drop one and pursue the other with dedication." Although I had completed my studies, I never made a serious effort to obtain a bachelor's degree in civil engineering or pursue a career in this field.

Despite being a traditional person, my father had no problem adapting to the needs of the times and technology. In 1996, I told him I wanted to launch a website called www.khosravani.com (which is still active today).

At that time, many institutions did not have websites. The evidence for this claim is that when we submitted the website advertisement for publication in the newspaper, they used the word "dot" instead of "." in the URL. Many banks still didn't have websites, and this was uncommon at the time. The domain was not yet available in Iran, so we purchased it from a Canadian company.

A Fraud Gang

During that time, several unfortunate incidents occurred. One of them involved a fraud gang called "Reza Kaboli," which operated under false names and addresses, dealing in buying and selling cars.

I fell into the trap of this fraudulent group once. With the savings I had, I purchased a Paykan car worth four million tomans from them. However, after a few days, the police intervened, took the Paykan from me, returned it to its rightful owner, and I found myself at a loss.

I remember my father, in terms of punishment, never compensated me for that money, which left me very upset because I had lost all my capital and savings accumulated over several years at once.

During those days, I worked hard. I only had a motorcycle, which I used to navigate through traffic. I would come from the car exhibition, roam around Jomhoori Square and Pasteur Street, then from Enqelab Square to Chubi Bridge, and visit all the car exhibitions in the city center. I was looking for suitable cars for buying and selling.

One could say that motorcycle was my first branch, and even after many years, I have kept it as a memento of those times. During the day, I would go to Iran Khodro's dealership, buy invoices, and at night, I would take some cars, line them up for numbering, and act as a proxy for others, handling their tasks. Despite my father not being poor, he didn't give me any money and only provided me with the opportunity to work.

Karim the Barber

I was so busy that I didn't have time to go to the barber. I remember that at 11 o'clock at night when I returned home, only one barber shop was open late, and a person named Karim was sweeping outside. One night, I had to entrust him to cut my hair short. The next day, everyone who saw me asked in amazement, "What happened, Ali? Did you just get released from prison? Why did you shave your head!" Although I knew Karim wasn't a good barber, I had no choice but to go to him due to my busy schedule, and for several months, I entrusted him with cutting my hair late at night.

Until one day, sooner than usual, I returned home and went to Karim's barber shop to get my hair cut. I noticed Karim standing in a corner, and two other people were cutting hair. That's when I realized Karim wasn't a barber at all. Karim was a worker at that shop, doing the cleaning, and he slept there at night! When it was my turn, the salon attendant asked me, "Who do you want to cut your hair with?" I said, "With Mr. Karim." Everyone laughed and thought I was joking with them. Later, I found out that the barbers in this salon were three brothers named Ahmad, Mahmoud, and Mohammad, and it is still operational. The salon had three chairs. One of the brothers, Ahmad, had left the job because he had been hired in an office. So, his chair was empty, and the other two brothers were looking for a replacement barber instead of Ahmad. When they realized that Mr. Karim had learned to cut hair and had become proficient, they assigned Ahmad's chair to him, and that's how Mr. Karim got the job, taking over Ahmad's chair.

Late at night, I would visit Karim, and we would sit together, sharing our joys and sorrows. He would talk to me about his love and how his family opposed his marriage. Fortunately, years later, he finally achieved his love and successfully married her, and now they have two children.

Years of hard work

During those years, all my concern was work. While most of my peers pursued recreational activities and hobbies, I was constantly working. I can't say whether this attitude is commendable or a flaw. But that was my disposition, and working excessively not only didn't upset me but was more enjoyable and pleasurable than anything else. Even now, between doing something recreational or work-related, I definitely prefer work. Even after I got married, my wife initially asked me with surprise, "Why don't you have friends of your age to socialize with and accompany us on trips or leisure activities?" She was right because since I entered this profession at a young age, most of my friends were work friends, and my type of relationship was work-related. Moreover, all my friends were older and more experienced.

After several years of continuous work and mastering all the ins and outs of the business, I became proud of myself and felt that the affairs of my father's shop were passing through me, and the wheel of his business was turning because of me. Therefore, I decided to separate.

Every day, I wanted to be independent and due to the connections, I had made, I was impatient to become independent. I found excuses for separating from Mr. Sohrab. Until one day, my father consented to this separation and said, "Now that you claim to be the one running our business, go work for yourself and leave us to our own devices."

In the years that followed, I realized that this was the biggest mistake of my life, and if I had the opportunity to go back to the past, I would never separate from my father. Because until that day, I was just a simple worker beside at my father's exhibition, and I had no idea about the troubles of being an employer and its complications. But after the separation, all the responsibilities fell on my shoulders, and I had to bear this heavy burden alone.

When I separated from my father, he provided me with two options:

1- My motorcycle.

2- Mc. Ahmad Bagher

Ahmad Bagher was our caretaker and had been with our family since childhood. Most of the time, he would take me to school and language classes and was somewhat like my guardian. My father said, "You can take Ahmad Bagher as your companion and family trustee." Because Ahmad Bagher had raised me since childhood, he had a hand in shaping my character, and my father knew he could be a good supporter and ally for me. My father knew that no one understood me as well as Ahmad

Bagher and knew how he could calm me down in times of anger and despair.

At that time, I didn't have more than forty million tomans in savings, and I knew that this amount wouldn't be enough to buy an exhibition. Therefore, I decided to buy an office. Establishing an office for buying and selling cars was not so popular at that time, and workshops were the top priority. Since I couldn't afford to buy an exhibition, I went to Azadi Street to buy an office. Then I came home and consulted with my father about the purchase.

My father was somewhat trusted and relied upon by all of us, and he is still the head of our trade union. Mr. Sohrab, after evaluating the situation of the office, said, "This office is not suitable for you because it has no room for progress and expansion." Therefore, he discouraged me from buying the office on Azadi Street. But the next night, he contacted me and said, "Come to Mr. Mohsen's workshop down the alley."

When I saw my father, he said, "I have found a place for you in Ayatollah Kashani Square, which seems suitable to me as a starting point, and it's feasible. You can start from this point." I asked, "How much is it?" He replied, "It's 850,000 tomans per square meter." The office space was about 90 square meters, and the total amount was around 73 million tomans. I didn't have enough money, about 30 million tomans, to buy this property.

Once again, my father acted in his own special way. Since he didn't want to cover the remaining amount for me, he introduced me to one of his friends, Mr. Hosseini, who was the manager of Parsian Bank in Zafar Branch. We went together to Parsian Bank, and he told his friend, "Ali wants to buy an apartment but is short of around 30 million tomans. Please lend him the money." At that time, banks offered loans with very high interest rates, close to 36 percent.

Eventually, with the loan, I was able to buy that unit. Mr. Sohrab also came and bought the neighboring unit. My mother was a bit surprised by my father's decision, saying, "Why are you buying this unit and spreading your capital around?" In those years, my father had spoken wisely to my mother and in response to her objection, he had said, "This young man. When he enters that building and the other neighbors realize that he owns two units in this building, they will treat him with more respect, and Ali will gain a special credibility."

In the following years, I realized that my father had invested in the adjacent unit for the advancement of my business, so that when I wanted to expand my business, I wouldn't face any problems in acquiring property. My father also bought four parking spaces in that complex and entrusted all the parking spaces to me, while renting out his own unit without a parking space to a tenant.

Generally, we received support from my father in this way, and Mr. Sohrab never directly gave us money. I always felt embarrassed about taking money directly from my father, and my father had his own way of giving money. For example, he would say, "Wash my car and put this amount in your pocket as your salary."

After buying the property, I changed the decoration to turn it into an office. After purchasing desks, chairs, and a television, I ran out of money. At that time, I had three employees. When one of my employees named "Fariborz Basiri" told me, "Ali, we need to buy a printer along with sugar and tea for the office." I replied, "Fariborz, I don't have any money left." I was truly penniless.

The next day, my father called me. He asked, "Do you have a Pride (a type of car)?" I said, "Let me check." I started calling and contacting various dealerships. I had a friend named "Saeed Moghadami Sepehr" on Dolat Street. He sold me a Pride for six million tomans. But I told Mr. Sohrab, "This red Pride will cost us six million and fifty thousand tomans." (It should be noted that at that time, fifty thousand tomans didn't make much of a difference financially, but it caused a lot of problems for me.) I'm sure my father understood at the time that this amount was very high, as he could easily unravel the situation with a phone call. However, he accepted it and said, "Okay. Come and get the money from me and buy the car for us." So I went and received the Pride and made a profit of fifty thousand tomans. Then I called Fariborz and said, "Come and take this fifty thousand tomans and go buy sugar, tea, a printer, and whatever else we need for the office immediately."

I spent hard and busy days. I had to pay 830 thousand tomans to the bank every month. All my days passed with stress. As the month progressed, I hustled to gather the money for the installment and the monthly salaries of the employees.

When I parted from my father, I felt like a severed branch, detached from the main tree and planted in a different soil to grow and thrive on its own. I was alone in a world full of installments and poverty. But I could still feel the support of Mr. Sohrab. Sometimes he would call my office and say, "Come and take these two cars and sell them in your office." I would immediately take the two cars and sell them, then buy two more cars from my father's dealership with the money. Finally, after three or four years, I managed to settle my debts with the bank.

Being Ali Khosravani

After much effort, I finally managed to establish myself in that office and somehow declare my independence to others. At that time, I used to advertise in Hamshahri newspaper, and the ads had to be under the name "Ali Khosravani" in Hamshahri newspaper. I wanted to assert my Ali-ness. Even now, many of my customers say, "We remember your ads with the name Ali Khosravani from thirty years ago." I put a lot of emphasis on this name and declaration of independence.

Although Mr. Sohrab did not give me any money, he did another great thing for me that propelled me several steps forward. He was entrusted to our guild, which is my son. If you borrow up to one billion tomans of goods from him, the commitment to repay is with me. But if the amount of his loans exceeds this amount, the commitment to the additional amount is not on me. Since I didn't have capital in circulation, apparently all the cars in the market were mine with this support from my father. With the trust and credibility of my father, I also respectfully carved out my place among my peers.

The important point was that I was not an ungrateful son, and I never exploited my father's credit for my personal interests. My father was very much a sound and honest man in his work. He taught us the technique of making money. His signature contributed to our growth and progress. He taught us that with respect and credibility, you can easily get money from people. He taught us that not only should we not take anything from others' tables, but we should also add something to people's tables. He is very healthy and honest in his field of activity, and even after years, he has maintained his position in this profession.

My father taught me well to move beyond money. To not be greedy in business and learn to bypass certain types of money so that later money would come after me. He was cautious about transactions and businesses that he knew were likely to run into legal trouble in the future, and he always earned his living in a halal and correct manner.

He had a famous saying that he always shared with me and my brother: "If you want your voice to carry weight, your attire must always be tidy. When you're not tainted by dirt, you can confidently speak out for your rights."

From that year until today, whenever we bought a car or closed a deal, we gathered with our employees, bought a cake, got a candle with a registration number, and took a commemorative photo. For instance, numbers like 106, 305, and 609.

When I settled into that office and managed to establish credibility for myself in the market, I expanded my staff. Due to limited space, I had to expand the office, so I purchased the adjacent unit owned by my father. While my father may have sold me the property at a five percent higher rate than the market, at that time, I realized that without this property from my father, I would have had to relocate and change the location of my office and workplace.

Auto Khosravani

After several years, we bought a few more units, and today that building is known as our central office. From the early days of establishing the office, I allocated a room as a training room. I felt that our work should move beyond traditional sales methods and become more modern. Therefore, I invited reputable professors of that time, such as Dr. Saheb and Dr. Kian, to come to our office and teach various training courses to me and my staff. For example, I took the DISC personality assessment course with Dr. Ahmadi. After completing these classes, I was able to recognize the different personalities of customers and advance in my work, knowing how to deal with desired customers based on different personality types such as logical, influential, duty-oriented, emotional, etc.

We learned sales techniques, negotiation skills, body language, verbal communication, telephone etiquette, personality profiling, psychology of personality, and other courses. I sent my salespeople to training classes to learn how to interact with customers and different personalities. I even sent company hosts to hospitality classes for a while to see hospitality techniques well. For example, they had to know that the handle of the tea cup should always face four o'clock. Or if a lady and a gentleman entered the office at the same time, they should first offer the tea cup to the lady. Or if a customer entered our company, the staff were not allowed to sit; they had to stand up and respectfully welcome the customer with a smile. Or if the staff were standing in front of the elevator and a customer wanted to take the elevator at the same time, they would first let the customer enter the elevator, press the parking button for them, and then stand aside and not accompany them downstairs.

Gradually, people noticed these differences. It was with these keywords that I established my own distinct style from the competition right from the start.

Finally, I managed to register my own brand in the car sales sector under the name "Auto Khosravani", which customers proudly mention when purchasing cars, even if they buy them at a higher price. I had achieved my goal because I was able to create an environment where customers proudly and completely satisfied announce everywhere that they bought our car from Khosravani. Even if someone else offers them a cheaper deal, the customer responds: "Well, I'm comfortable knowing that I've bought a reliable car."

Even the second-hand market sells our cars at a higher price compared to market rates. As soon as they see the second-hand sales contract, those who buy and sell cars after me offer them at a higher price because sellers and dealers are confident that the car was purchased from Auto Khosravani, so there are no defects in the product, and it doesn't have any manual options.

Imported Cars

After several years, I felt the need for my business to gain formal recognition. Following the opening of car imports, I secured the dealership for Ramak Car products. At this stage, we presented ourselves quite differently. Given the predominance of professionalism in the car industry, I extended invitations to anyone capable of imparting new insights or unique perspectives in this field to collaborate with us.

One day, I heard a valuable phrase from Dr. Kian that served as a source of inspiration for me and somewhat altered my thought process. He said: "Through my profession, I have collaborated with all brand owners and notable individuals, and I have come to realize that each brand and product possesses its unique signature, with their lasting impression lying in their distinctive mark. The traces of creativity and innovation are evident in these distinctions."

Reflecting on this phrase, I questioned myself: Where does my signature lie in the automotive industry, and how can I distinguish myself?

I ensured that everyone treated customers with kindness, prompting others to immediately remark: "This is the Khosravani way of doing things." It could be said that being kind and providing more value to customers than others has become my signature. I allowed customers to reach out to me under any circumstances and for any reason. For instance, a customer once called me at half past midnight, saying, "Mr. Khosravani, excuse me, but my car has a flat tire on Shariati Street." While others might argue that a flat tire is unrelated to us, in our office, it's a different story. When our salesperson hands over their card to the buyer, they say, "You can contact us 24/7." I tell the customer to call me for anything, even if they're going on a trip. It could be said that I have made the customer excessively comfortable and reliant on me.

My product

The crucial point here is that my product isn't a car and isn't currently a car. Since I don't engage in manufacturing, the car I have here is also available in other showrooms.
In fact, my product is **the process of purchasing a car safely.**
My product is **the hassle-free process of selling a car.**
Therefore, I don't need to advertise the car's quality. It's the manufacturer's responsibility to promote the quality of their product, not mine. My role is to assist you if you wish to purchase a car:
Firstly, I will assess to determine which product is suitable for you based on your budget, living conditions, family size, and usage requirements for the car.
Secondly, I will help you to buy your desired car model without any hassle and in a very comfortable manner.
In the car sales industry, we have deprioritized the discussion of

cars and shifted our focus. We have decided to become effective consultants.

We have trained our staff on how to earn the trust of customers and how to sell a car. We do not have subpar cars here. In my opinion, the Pride is a suitable option for someone who is an employee and cannot spend more than necessary on their family's car expenses each month. However, if we decide to drive the Pride at 180 km/h and cause an accident, the responsibility lies with us, not the Pride car.

We cannot tell a customer who can only afford to spend two hundred million tomans on a car that "the Pride car is useless and only a BMW is worth driving." Therefore, any customer who enters our showroom, if we determine that the car is not suitable for them, we refrain from selling it to them.

For example, if a young person comes to our office and says, "I want a car, something around two billion tomans," and I know this young person goes off-roading every week and the cost of the car is not a significant factor for them, I would definitely offer them a 20-year-old Roniz off-road car. However, if a teacher comes to us and says they have 800 million tomans with a fixed monthly income, I would never recommend a Roniz car to them; instead, I would suggest a good Chinese car that fits their budget and comes with a five-year warranty.

Thirteen Brands

After entering the realm of dealership and obtaining the necessary licenses, we acquired representations for numerous brands.

I had around thirteen brand representations. Brands such as BMW, Mitsubishi, Hyundai, Kia Motors, and others. In the sale of all these products, I achieved the first rank in representation. Personally, I prefer to be eighth in my work, but not second. My taboo is coming in second. I believe that a person should always strive to be first in whatever they do. For example, you know the name of the first person in the world's two sprint fields very well, "Usain Bolt." And it's always the name of the first person in sports fields that audiences remember worldwide, not the second person. Do you know the name of the second person in the world's two sprint fields? While the difference between first and second place is only in fractions of a second.

- The secret to being first and staying at the top lies in that final effort.
- The secret to being first and staying at the top lies in attention to detail and meticulousness.
- The secret to being first and staying at the top lies in recognizing differences and making your own unique signature.

Prominent Examples at Auto Khosravani

After a while, we realized that providing 24/7 customer service was a general concept for us, and we needed finer examples for our unique signature at Auto Khosravani. Therefore, we decided to offer different conditions and services to customers at Auto Khosravani. For example, if you buy a SsangYong from us, our company offers you a one-year free replacement warranty in addition to the warranty period provided by the dealership.

This means that if you encounter any issues with the car in the first year, we'll take back the faulty car and provide you with a brand new one, without charging a single extra dime.

When I defined these special conditions at Auto Khosravani, instead of competing with me and trying to score higher, my competitors all admitted, "Ali Khosravani is lying and it's impossible for him to replace a brand-new car in the first year of purchase if any issues arise." However, after this incident, when one of our customers was offered such a service, competitors acknowledged the truth themselves.

If you search the news archives, you'll see that there's an article about our company regarding the defective car replacement section.

When I was introduced as the first rank in the sales excellence ceremony at Milad Tower, Mr. Ghafourian approached me and sarcastically said, "I don't know why Mr. Khosravani, you're not so active in the after-sales service aspect, unlike others?" In response, I said to him, "What's your definition of after-sales service? Is it enough just to lift a car's four wheels for a customer?!"

I also suggested to him, "It's better if you bring the customers to whom you've provided after-sales services, and I'll bring those who, instead of services, have received a brand-new car from our company after reporting engine or gearbox defects, so we can compare and see which group is more satisfied!"

Interestingly, when I propose an idea, everyone initially ridicules me because they see no logical justification for it in their view.

Personally, whenever I want to implement a new idea to advance my work, I first discuss it with a few people. The more opponents there are, the more firmly I pursue that idea. Because I believe that if the idea occurred to me, and it occurred to others too, then it's no longer a unique idea.

I'm always pursuing tasks that seem impossible to turn them into reality. Most of the time, because others can't comprehend or digest my unconventional ideas, they ridicule me.

In fact, I derive more pleasure from customer satisfaction than profitability. Since I needed advertising material, let me share a story in this regard: One day, a customer called our receptionist and said, 'My car's gearbox is making noise.' When Milad, our marketing manager, spoke to the customer and after some inquiries, he assured them, 'Don't worry, you have a replacement warranty, and we'll replace your car tomorrow.' The customer, astonished, exclaimed over the phone, 'No sir, my car's condition isn't severe enough to require replacement, and perhaps the problem isn't even with the gearbox!'

Most customers find it hard to believe that we go to such lengths in replacing a defective car. This approach became my signature and earned me the necessary credibility. Interestingly, because of this warranty, I was brought to the attention of the Consumer Protection Organization, who asked, 'Under what authority do you offer such a warranty to your customers?' In response, I said, 'Instead of hindering my work, you should also enforce this for other sellers.'

When this discussion arose, I told the staff there, 'I offer this warranty to the customer, and you cannot interfere with my work. But if after providing this warranty, I fail to deliver the promised services, the customer can complain against me. Then you can reprimand me, but not now when you want to punish before the crime.

Other competitors lodged numerous complaints against me, claiming that Khosravani's approach undersells our customers and harms our sales. This was while they had complete freedom for after-sales services in their own agencies and could provide any service under their after-sales warranty.

Tivoli at Palladium Shopping Center

We were the first company to bring cars to shopping centers, and we introduced Tivoli to the Palladium commercial center. Mr. Raftering, the Palladium manager, had to change the entrance door because of our product delivery. They spent thirty million tomans that year to showcase Tivoli and make the entrance bigger.

I also booked some seats at Café Viona for customers coming to see Tivoli at Palladium. We treated VIP guests at the Spio restaurant in the shopping center too. Mr. Raftari, who later became a friend, said, "Khosravani, I got worried." I asked, "Why?" He said, "When you registered a thousand Tivoli here, it somehow tied our fate. If the company fails to deliver these cars on time, unhappy customers will come to me first, and then to you!"

I chuckled and said, "Mr. Raftari, you've tried every way to make money. Now, let's try making money from showcasing cars together

After crossing this milestone, Mr. Raftari, the owner of Palladium center, trusted us more and we became close friends. Following our success, other dealerships also brought their cars to Palladium for display, turning it into a new income source for them.

Another thing I did for Tivoli was to sponsor its advertisements on the JAM network, without mentioning Auto Khosravani. Some acquaintances questioned me, "Why are you spending money on promoting Tivoli without mentioning Auto Khosravani?" In response, I explained, "I own 25% of Tivoli's national sales. It's like owning 25% of a field, with the remaining 75% divided among 60 other people. If I focus on my 25% and ensure timely watering, I'll profit more than the other 60 people.

Test Drive

In our car industry, the concept of a test drive doesn't exist. Why? Because we never saw a reason to convince people to come and buy our cars. So, you never saw a time when Iran Khodro wanted to produce a car (for example, in 2000 when they introduced the Persia) and sent a sample to every dealership, asking people to ride in this car model to see if they feel satisfied and enjoy it or not.

Unfortunately, customer opinion has never been important or considered by Iranian manufacturers in the automotive industry. This top-down view still exists and persists in the automotive industry.

In my opinion, when destiny led me into the car sales profession, they wanted me to break this kind of view in society. I thought to myself, now that I'm inevitably in the car sales profession, I have two choices: Either accept this volume of criticism against car salesmen and leave or stay and change this perspective.

My goal was to take the automotive sector from point A to point B. Certainly, after me, reaching other points C and D will also be discussed, and the creative minds of the youth will develop it. But one thing is for sure, no one can start from point A anymore. Society's mindset has changed, and in every field, it must be accompanied by the needs of society and new definitions.

Anyway, I told the company: "Give me three cars on installments so that I can put them in a test drive." The company didn't agree and refused to give the cars for testing.

So, I had to buy three cars myself and tell customers, "If, for example, you want to buy a Tivoli, you can test drive it before buying. Come to me and test drive this car model, but can go somewhere else to register. You have no restrictions on testing the car.

This is where my art of attracting customers manifested through the training I provided to my staff.

We had three types of flash drives at Auto Khosravani: pink, green, and grey. Each of these flash drives was suitable for a specific age group: young, middle-aged, and elderly. Pink was for those under 30, green for ages 30 to 55, and taupe for those 55 and older.

Our salespeople would act in the following manner when facing a customer: based on their perception and what they observed from the customer, they would select the flash drive appropriate for the customer's age. These flash drives contained music suitable for different ages and moods. For example, hip-hop songs for young people, Faramarz Aslani's songs for middle-aged individuals, and nostalgic and classic songs for the elderly were stored on the flash drives.

Secondly, during the visit and test drive, the salesperson subtly had to determine whether the customer was tactile, visual, or auditory. If they couldn't discern, they would implement all three options on the customer. If the person was tactile, they would ask them to touch the car or sit in the driver's seat and test it. The car always had to smell good and be clean and shiny. At the same time, the customer's preferred music would be played, and without realizing it, the customer would purchase their desired car.

If a customer doesn't make a purchase from us and leaves after the test drive, the fault lies with us, not the customer. It's because we failed to attract them. I tell our staff, "Never blame the customer; it's our lack of persuasiveness that prevents us from convincing them to buy."

We tried other techniques too. We announced that anyone purchasing from our branches would be entered into a year-end celebration where we would raffle off a Tivoli car as a prize. We followed through with this and held the celebration at the Fakhr Razi Conference Center of Iran University of Medical Sciences, with famous comedians and singers in attendance.

We can't afford not to fulfill our promises. In this competitive environment where competitors are keen to exploit any weaknesses and find excuses, failing to deliver on even one promise would immediately brand us as dishonest.

Next, we entered into a contract with Snapp driving service, and by giving out codes, we facilitated free rides for customers who wanted to visit our branches.

Once, someone said to me, "You're so naive, I overheard someone saying, 'You have no idea how easy it is to outsmart Khosravani. Since my mother's house is near the Niavaran St. branch, whenever I want to visit her, I take a free ride with Khosravani's Snapp code, walk a few steps past the branch, and I'm at my mother's house." In response, I said, "That's enough for me. Because the cost of that Snapp ride to me is not that much of a loss, but having someone sit down and mention the Khosravani name and the Niavaran St. branch in gatherings of ten to twenty people serves as free and cost-effective advertising for me.

After that, we entered into a contract with a flower distribution company to send a beautifully arranged bouquet of roses to our customers' doorsteps after their purchase.

In the automotive industry exhibition held a few years ago, we applied for a booth. Initially, our request was rejected, with the organizers stating, "This is an automotive industry exhibition, and all booths are reserved for well-known brands and manufacturers." Without asking for any explanation from us or reviewing how our services would be presented, they rejected our request outright. With persistence and diplomacy, I attended a meeting where the head of the exhibition organizers was present that year. I said to the head, "I have something to say in the distribution field. My story is about distribution, and I'm not a manufacturer. Your exhibition is also an automotive industry exhibition, and you should provide a booth to one of the largest distributors in this industry. Eventually, I managed to persuade them, and I obtained a booth in the Persian Gulf Hall of the exhibition. During this period, everyone was amazed to see the extensive interest in our booth, unlike the other booths. I provided services to customers such as test drives, car replacement warranties, and product introductions. We had a showman, singers, and even set up a news studio where we presented car sales news to the audience. All the reporters were drawn to our booth. We also organized a comedy program called "Dr. Esharaki, the Former Fesharaki." This comedy program featured Dr. Esharaki, who humorously presented automotive events of the day to the visitors. I wrote the scripts for this program myself and handed them to the performers for presentation. At this very exhibition, we earned the top ranking from the customer's perspective. We shone so brightly at this exhibition that we were invited to participate in the exhibition the following year.

Car Club

In 2017, we organized the "Car Club" event at the Milad Tower's three halls. Car Club was Iran's first disco-themed car event without alcohol.

Car Club was a car-themed party that I intended to organize. Thirteen thousand people attended the event in these halls. Renowned artists were present in the special guest section. In another section, there was a children's theater, and on the other side, children could paint and participate in educational activities. Special receptions accompanied by dinner were held. We organized fun competitions and games with special prizes. We conducted extensive advertising, and even after several years, no company or organization has been able to organize such an event in Iran. We still use the data and contacts from those who participated in this club and collaborate with them in various situations.

In this club, we introduced all the companies for which we were responsible for sales representation and showcased their products. Each brand had a fully professional presenter who introduced the products with displays and catalogs.

All the journalists who attended this club admitted that the level of this car club was much higher than that of many automotive exhibitions held in various cities across the country.

Personally, I meticulously supervised every detail of setting up the exhibition and sometimes stayed up all night, standing shoulder to shoulder with the organizers, ensuring everything was in order.

We had hired a marketing consultant, and wherever a car event was held, we were also present. For example, when the Mitsubishi PHEV (Plug-in Hybrid Electric Vehicle) was unveiled, they entrusted me with the first fully electric car. To attract the exhibition audience, I organized a Sushi and Mitsubishi festival simultaneously. I set aside the car discussion and, instead, invited a Japanese dance group that was present at the Japanese embassy in Iran to perform at the exhibition along with serving Japanese sushi. The exhibition received widespread acclaim because combining car advertising with the promotion of Japanese culture and cuisine had a significant impact on attracting and engaging customers, resulting in Mitsubishi selling far beyond our expectations.

Social Responsibility

In the realm of social responsibility, we expanded our activities. For example, we would release prisoners of unintentional and financial crimes on occasions like Ramadan. In various celebrations such as Yalda Night and Norouz, with appropriate designs and offerings, we attracted them more than ever to Autokhosravani. We managed to become the country's top car seller.

I believe I can only be the first in competition. Contrary to popular belief that this monopoly on cars, inflation, and high prices have propelled me forward, I must admit that I can be the first and have become so in a competitive environment. Because I used to say, if you buy a car from me, I'll give you these benefits. Competitors had to offer higher benefits to attract my customers. Personally, I despise non-competitive environments and love competition. I believe the absence of such an environment in society leads to stagnation and business obsolescence. Until 2018-2019 and even in the years before that, we were ranked as the top car seller under the Autokhosravani brand. We sold 12,600 and 12,400 cars in two years. After major car companies, we were the largest car seller in Iran. Even at the SsangYong exhibition in South Korea, our agency and company had sold more cars than seventy percent of other companies. While the country had sold 1700 cars, our dealership alone managed to sell 2700 cars.

Our major problem was that our only competitor was ourselves, and we had to come up with new and amazing ideas to evaluate ourselves. We set records for ourselves. Everyone says Mr. Takhti was unbeatable in wrestling. But I say if Khairallah Amiri, Takhti's teammate and sparring partner, wasn't there, this wrestler wouldn't have been recognized to this extent. While Khairallah Amiri was also a very talented and skilled wrestler like Takhti, no one saw him, and this wrestler, in a way, became a sacrificed for Takhti's fame and glory.

The Prohibition of Car Imports

In the year car imports were banned in Iran, our company's situation took a drastic turn, resembling a sand hourglass flipped upside down. We found ourselves amidst the highest levels of risk-taking. Many company CEOs were imprisoned, and numerous businesses went bankrupt. As for selling various car models, I faced the most significant challenges among all companies because I had the highest sales figures. In such circumstances, I reminded myself that when I took on the responsibility of representing these companies, I had to accept all the consequences. Just as in good times, I enjoyed many benefits from this path, now in these difficult times, I had to endure all the troubles. Customers would come, vent their frustrations at me, and then leave, never reaching the central office. Because if they did reach the main tent, they would dismantle it, causing disruption for our entire industry."

On one hand, I faced the most backlash and dissatisfaction, and on the other hand, customers, due to Auto Khosravani's high credibility, wanted to leverage their position to gain special privileges from us. They were rightfully upset because they had paid the pre-purchase amount for their cars at the rate of 4200 Tomans per dollar, and now they had to receive their cars at a much higher exchange rate.

To address these complaints, I hired five lawyers. I also hired a motorcycle courier to deliver messages to various branches. My desk was placed in the middle of the exhibition hall. I dealt with all sorts of personalities. Some were logical, some were agitated and abusive. My staff and I had to adapt to each personality and communicate accordingly.

For example, a customer had come, paid two hundred million for the pre-purchase of a certain Japanese car at the rate of 4200 Tomans per dollar, and now that the exchange rate had reached 16000, the government was pressuring us to cover the shortfall from the customer's pocket. Customers constantly berated us, regardless of the fact that this extra cost did not come out of our pockets and went directly to the government.

I endured a very difficult period and became mentally ill. I would put two sleeping pills and two tranquilizers next to my bed every night. Due to the intensity of the stress, I would wake up from sleep every few hours. I would sweat so much that it felt like someone had poured a bucket of water over me, and I had to change my pillow and clothes.

Despite the challenges, I persevered until the end, emerging from this ordeal unscathed. During this period, while most of our competitors shuttered their operations, we stood firm and didn't disband our dealerships.

Staying true to our principles

Prior to the ban on car imports, my business followed a straightforward routine: customers would come to me, register a vehicle, and after delivery, I'd receive my commission and hand over the car. However, under the new circumstances, this option was stripped from us, and I had to ensure the rights and livelihoods of my employees and staff. It was here that reconnecting with my roots proved instrumental in guiding me through.

As Rumi famously said:

"Whoever remains distant from their essence will seek to reconnect with it again."

I inherently understood the art of car salesmanship. I had mastered the knowledge of selling cars entirely and knew exactly how to go about it. I always used to tell my staff, "You won't stay with me forever. From a certain point onward, you need to find your own path and start your desired business. I always told my employees, "You won't stay with me forever. Therefore, from a certain point onwards, you must find your own path and start your desired business."

I had an employee named Mr. Zahrayi, who initially joined our company as a motorcycle courier. On his first day at the office, I saw him carrying an extra raincoat because he had predicted that if it rained today, he wouldn't get cold while riding his motorcycle. Right then and there, I said to myself, "This person is progressing in his work because he is very detail-oriented and forward-thinking." And so, it happened. Zahrayi gradually progressed and became the office manager. When his financial situation improved, he bought a Pride car and one day he said to me, "Mr. Khosravani, I want to sell my motorcycle." I said, "Never sell your motorcycle." He asked, "Why?" I replied, "Even if a carpenter becomes the owner of a wood factory, he never sells his saw and hammer." The future is unpredictable, and one day you might need that same motorcycle again. Never sell the primary tools of your expertise at any cost.

After this advice, I also returned to my essence. We started buying and selling cars again. I told myself, "As long as there is asphalt on the streets, there will be cars. If Mitsubishi and BMW don't enter the market, then there are still Pride and Peugeot cars, and we can keep the company afloat by selling them.

On one hand, every year from early July to September, I taught all the ins and outs of sales in my training classes. After three months of internship, if the intern could meet the predetermined sales target in the first three months, they would stay with the company and continue working here.

A New Challenge

A new challenge, however, arose for me during this period, as I had some corporate salespeople. Corporate salespeople are essentially operators and not salespeople. I would tell them, "Don't think you are great salespeople. If I put a message recorder behind my phone line, it could sell ten cars by the end of the day. In my opinion, a salesperson who can't grasp the market pulse isn't a salesperson."

In these circumstances, we introduced a new technique in supply and sales. We convinced a customer who came to us to register their desired car to register for two cars instead of one. After purchasing, by selling the receipt of one of them, we would procure the rest of the money for their second car. This was like when someone sitting in a restaurant orders Baghali polo with meat (a traditional Iranian dish), selling him a drink wouldn't be too difficult

In my opinion, anyone in their role can be a good salesperson. For example, a teacher, a dentist, and others can be good salespeople because they've managed to bring their students or patients back to their classrooms or clinics. When you can attract your customers, satisfy their tastes and spirits, and persuade them to buy or stay, you are a successful salesperson.

You must always be a servant and helper of the people. In sales, you have to be humble yet very clever and smart.

In this particular period, we had to transform the corporate style into a peddler's style because the corporate style wasn't about providing consultancy to the customer. They presented the specific product in their own way and focused more on financial aspects and profitability in sales. But the style of selling cars is different. The buyer knows what they want, and the dealer must be able to convince the seller to sell. This is while in the corporate style, the desired car is obtained through the company's intermediary.

Now, I was faced with a number of corporate salespeople who were not familiar with the peddler's style. I had to teach them all the points from the beginning. I had to teach them techniques for bargaining or procurement. They had to practice handwriting, social etiquette, customer interaction, and dealing with the boss in front of the mirror.

After teaching the peddler's style to the staff, I immediately contacted old customers and markets and said, "If anyone buys a used car from us, we provide a one-year warranty for the engine and gearbox." Because the challenge for people in the used car market is about services, we also provided a warranty for used cars after sales.

It seems like other companies also copied our methods. For example, when I approached Arian Motor Company to become their representative, I told them to give me a three-month dealership, and if my sales were poor, they could cancel the contract. Within just five months, I quickly rose to the top spot in Mitsubishi sales. Some companies copied our business model and strategies, but they weren't successful because their focus was on a single brand, and they lacked expertise in multi-brand operations and selling used cars.

Salespeople Production Factory

With this new approach, after a short period, our company transformed into a "salespeople factory." It was like everyone was talking about my staffs and even the janitor was wanted by other companies. All the salespeople at Auto Khosravani became so skilled that all companies wanted to hire them because they knew they could handle sales under any circumstances. Even now, every year, a new spectrum of job applicants enters this organization, while another spectrum exits. I implemented this style of work and gained another distinguishing feature.

Competition on the International Stage

Ater a while, I realized that continuing in this manner was no longer beneficial, as we were consistently ranking first nationally every year. If we didn't measure ourselves in higher and international arenas, then remaining at the top was meaningless. Being first in sales every year had become a major liability for us. So, we pondered what to do to become enduring in another field. How could we safeguard ourselves from governmental decisions?

To continue in this profession, I had to either compromise my principles and go along with the system or find a way to establish lasting presence in this industry. Since conforming and giving in didn't align with my values, I decided to stay and strive for longevity. In fact, facing setbacks became part of my daily life, and I grew and evolved through these failures, as I have done thus far.

Gap in the Service Sector

When I noticed a significant gap in the service sector, I decided to offer my own special and unique services in this field.

In 2018, amidst currency and inflation challenges, our financial manager said, 'We need to downsize thirty percent of the staff.' Since our income source had been obliterated, we were at a dead end. Financial matters, being solely about numbers, have little regard for delicate emotions. Unlike the company's financial manager, I couldn't easily digest this decision. Moreover, throughout all these years, no one had ever complained to the labor office about being fired or leaving Autokhosravani Company, and I had never faced any legal challenges from that office.

I was confused and didn't know what decision to make. So, I gathered all Autokhosravani staff together and announced: 'I have to reduce thirty percent of you.' So, we had two options:
 Thirty percent of you leave the company voluntarily or all of us, including myself, accept thirty percent lower salaries so we can continue together.

It was decided to proceed based on a secret ballot and the collective decision. The staff said, 'There's no need for a secret ballot. We'll all take thirty percent less, but we'll still be here together.'

With this unity, just two months later, our income, mine and the staff's, was thirty percent less than before, and by the third month, our earnings returned to the previous level. We had made a big decision together, and each one of us showed extraordinary sacrifice for the sake of the others.

A few years ago, the tax office targeted us. We had to take down the Autokhosravani website. We downsized our staff and lowered our level to escape tax pressure. Mr. Kavousi led the tax group of my company. I told him, 'You're taking heavy taxes from me for advertising, while you well know our company's income isn't that high. Don't judge me based on this advertising because someone who advertises a lot clearly still needs to attract customers.' In response to my objection, Mr. Kavousi said, 'Don't fool me. If there are five big car sellers in Tehran, you're one of them.' At that time, I wasn't even considered among the top fifty car sellers in Tehran!

This statement from Mr. Kavousi hit me hard, and when I left the tax office, I told the staff, 'Bring the website back up. Get everything organized. We need to expand our business. When people look at me from the outside, they say you're one of the best, so why pretend I'm not? This isn't me!'

We had to make every effort to reach the top level. Later, my brother Hossein joined us and became part of Autokhosravani. One morning, my phone rang early. Seeing my brother's name, I answered with concern. Hossein said to me, 'Ali, I'm in trouble. I have to pay a billion in taxes.' I said, 'Congratulations to you.' He asked, 'Why?' I said, every success comes with its own challenges. I congratulate you on entering the club of taxpayers with a billion. Instead of finding a way to reduce this tax amount, expand your business in a way that you can easily pay ten billion in taxes. Get yourself to a point where a billion is just a stepping stone for you.

The Story of "AutoShenas"

As I've mentioned before, from a certain point onward, I had to either gracefully retire like the champions and bid farewell to the pinnacle of the world of champions, or if I wanted to remain in the competition, I had to establish a new space. In fact, the factor that hindered car imports to Iran was a wake-up call for us to change our path. At this juncture, I wanted to do something to ensure the Khosravani name remained in the automotive sector and stayed enduring for years to come.

When we had excelled in the car sales sector and were advancing without competitors, I asked myself: What's next after this? Where are we supposed to go from here? If we didn't embrace a new approach, we wouldn't have durability, and we would be forced to leave the scene with failure.

Since my spirit was one of challenge, and I couldn't settle for mediocrity, and also because I wanted this brand to endure, when I explored various sectors like manufacturing, I realized I didn't have the production spirit and couldn't enter this realm. I would have to start from zero point, and besides, the manufacturing environment in our country wasn't conducive.

But after researching the service sector, I realized there were countless deficiencies and shortcomings, and the level of service to the people was very low. In this sector, there's a top-down attitude towards the customer and consumer. Car manufacturers don't feel obligated to be responsive to the customer or attract them. After conducting research, I initially concluded that in the after-sales service sector, we could elevate customer satisfaction through creative solutions. I realized that by establishing a repair shop and incorporating a clean sanitary service, with only soap and paper towels provided, we could potentially rank first nationwide. I make this comparison to highlight the existing weaknesses in this sector in our country for the esteemed readers to understand.

Therefore, I decided to elevate post-sales services to an international level. In the first step, I closely examined about seventy automotive service companies worldwide. In various places like Dubai, Turkey, Georgia, North America, and others, I studied various centers and diverse brands.

In the second step, I defined the needs of the Iranian market and saw that we are weak in two aspects in the automotive service sector in Iran: 1- Trust 2- Respect.

The first problem: Customers do not trust car service centers and constantly think that they are replacing original car parts with low-quality aftermarket parts.

The second problem: Service providers do not show the necessary respect towards customers. Respect is not only about smiling and being polite; it means that a space for customer comfort is not provided during their presence at service centers. These services should be defined based on customer needs, and sufficient explanations were not given to the customers. Also, offering a fair price is considered part of respecting the customer. For example, we would take the car of a surgeon from their home early in the morning before they go to the hospital, and after completing the services, we would return the car to their clinic in the evening. Or if we took a lady's car from her home parking lot in the morning, we would deliver it to her desired location, such as a shop center where she had gone for shopping. Until recently, we did not have a widespread brand of high-quality services in the automotive sector in Iran. We had restaurant brands, clothing brands, but we did not have such a brand in the automotive sector, and its absence was strongly felt. For example, in areas such as oil change for cars, we did not have standardized services, but they existed elsewhere in the world. Considering what I had seen in different countries and the needs of our society, I launched a service company called "AutoShenas," which was an Iranianized version of the models I had seen abroad. We tried to meet all the needs of Iranian customers in this company.

In the matter of gaining customer trust, we also focused on personnel branding. Now that the customer has trusted us, our professional integrity does not allow us to deceive. My presence on social networks has made me always under scrutiny and cautious not to allow anyone to throw a stone towards the glass walls of the house I've built around myself. I have expanded the infrastructure of my work so much that I cannot afford the slightest mistake to preserve these foundations.

At Auto Khosravani, we noticed that our car attendants were lacking professionalism at some point, and after a while, we realized that we had a problem in the car attendant department.

What does that mean? It means that we put in a lot of effort to bring the customer into the establishment and then put in a lot of effort to do the selling, but when the order was sent to the doorstep, this person, with their unprofessional behavior or by providing incorrect and misleading information, would undermine our credibility!

Therefore, I gathered the car attendants and with the help of a friend, we decided to change their tone and style. We decided to teach them twenty key phrases. Phrases like: "Is there anything else I can assist you with?" or "Thank you for your support and..."

In the next step, we sent them all to a dental clinic to follow up on their dental health. We dressed them in clean and uniform clothes. We provided them with a protocol that required their cars to be fully fueled at the time of delivery. The car had to be clean and presentable.

In the next stage, the car attendant had to ask the buyer: "May I park the car for you?" Also, after delivering the car, they had to provide necessary explanations to the buyer and finally ask them: "Do you have any further questions?"

We also trained these drivers on the car's options so that they could ask the buyer if they were familiar with the options or needed an explanation after encountering the buyer. They were also able to provide explanations to the customer about the service card, document follow-ups, and parts replacement. And finally, they would give their own card to the customer and say: "If you have any issues, you can contact us 24/7."

We instilled this level of responsibility in our car attendants. They had to learn crisis management and provide customer satisfaction calmly by delivering key phrases.

As the type of business in Iran was changing towards the startup space, we also had to adapt to a new style of work. Even though we could have continued with the classic style of Auto Khosravani, we would quickly fall behind the prevailing style in society, to our detriment.

Currently, the goal of many service companies in Iran is to reach the position we had in the classic era of Auto Khosravani. Therefore, to stay ahead of the competition, we needed to align our services with the current conditions of society. So, we designed a native software application.

Nowadays, from beginning to end, car services are done at AutoShenas, and the services are divided into several major sections:

- Specialized workshop services
- Buying and selling
- Body, technical, authenticity and engine expertise
- Cover, ceramic, and detailing
- AutoBar emergency services

Next, we examined the shortcomings:

1. One of these deficiencies was the issue of expertise. Nowadays, the online space has taken over traditional businesses. Essentially, these platforms have hijacked our business, and we had to reach the level of these platforms. The necessary exper-

tise here was that after choosing their car through platforms in the virtual space, the customer needed someone or a company in the real world to confirm their purchase. The area of expertise in the new style of buying and selling was somewhat narrowed down. For example, in Canada, through dealerships (which are administrative papers from government-designated centers), the buyer knows what car they are purchasing, along with its advantages and disadvantages. Workshops also issue this paper and present it to the customer. The seller, buyer, and expert are all trusted and respected in their respective positions. Therefore, we also created the expertise issue at AutoShenas, and based on our own expertise, we sell the car to the customer.

2. On the other hand, the issue of roadside cars was raised. At AutoShenas, we introduced the concept of "AutoYar" and provide services in the best possible way, often free of charge. We also offer internet taxis for drivers whose cars have problems and provide free refueling. We provide innovative services in the field of roadside assistance.

3. In the "AutoUp" area, the issue of car care also emerged. Until a few years ago, covering cars was mostly for young people and considered uncommon act. But with the erratic rise in car prices, more people are now seeking these services. New covers prevent scratches and damage. We have also established reputable agencies in this field.

4. We expanded our activities in the academy sector as well. We launched AutoYar and promoted the training issue. Anyone who

wants to engage in a profession must learn it experientially from zero point to mastery. Our salespeople come from high apprenticeship to sales positions.

5. In the women's sector, we realized that the environment of repair shops does not provide psychological security for women. That is, if a woman wanted to go to a repair shop, either her husband accompanied her or they prevented her from going alone. Therefore, we created a suitable space to provide peace of mind and psychological safety for women.

6. We also launched the "Auto Café" brand. We created an environment where customers can enjoy their time in a chic and professional Auto Cafe while servicing their cars, accompanied by friends or companions.

Entrepreneurship

At a certain point, I couldn't work for money anymore. I told myself: "If you want to continue your profession, money shouldn't be the main concern, and you should pursue a stronger motivation."

In my opinion, the existence of an increasing rate of inflation has damaged our country's human resources by promoting the spirit of getting rich.

Today, at AutoShenas, we have launched free training and entrepreneurship initiatives for young people. Entrepreneurship, to me, isn't just about getting a job; it's about finding joy in seeing our students succeed after their training. For me, the moment of taking flight is beautiful, even if the bird flies out of sight.

Our goal at AutoShenas is to become a renowned brand in Iran, provided we adhere to global standards and provide services to our customers based on these standards.

Currently, we have three branches in operation, and soon we will launch three more branches in the coming months. We aim to move towards franchising.

My concern for the development of AutoShenas is ensuring that my human resources embody the culture of AutoShenas. They must embrace the mental culture of AutoShenas because, in Iran, admitting mistakes is rare, and we are always justifying ourselves. Therefore, my human resources must take the lead with customers and proudly represent our values.

I want customers to recognize, solely from the way our staff behaves and communicates, that they are receiving services from AutoShenas. I don't want them to remember AutoShenas just because of a logo or a specific color.

Technically, we don't have many problems in Iran. Our challenge is more cultural. We are often weak in customer orientation, and I hope we can elevate this aspect to the highest level at AutoShenas.

I hope that in the future, when it comes to car services, everyone will acknowledge that Khosravani established the right approach in this field with AutoShenas.

Memorable Car Accident

I once stated that we cannot prevent accidents, and this is almost impossible. However, let's make this accident cost-effective for the customer. I gathered insurance representatives and told them, "Let's make the accident a memorable experience for the customer by providing respectful, easy, and quick services. By offering a replacement car until their damaged car is repaired, we ensure that during the repair time, customers can still carry on with their activities using another car. The plan "Repair today, pay next month."

Upon careful examination, I realized that we don't accept Visa or Mastercard here in Iran, making it difficult for customers to use these services comfortably, especially in tough economic conditions. For instance, if a Hyundai Santa Fe car gets into an accident, it could cost the owner at least 300 million Tomans. Therefore, I suggested that anyone who brings their car here for repairs can pay the expenses a month later. While a customer might be able to pay the repair costs upfront without any issues, by offering this service, I assure the customer of the quality of our services. It creates financial flexibility for the customer, and if they can't afford the repair costs immediately after an accident, they can sell their repaired car at a higher price and settle their account with us later.

The "Peidow" Plan

Every day at 2 p.m., Peidow Company sends its fuel car to AutoShenas to fill the tanks of all our repair cars with gasoline.

The "Acibadem" Law

This is a law that I have defined for myself, based on my personal experiences. The name originates from the time when I got sick in Turkey and went to "Acibadem" Hospital in Istanbul for treatment. Upon arrival, the reception nurse explained to me: "The procedure in this hospital is as follows: first, we collect 600 liras from you as an entrance fee. After the doctor examines you, it will be determined whether you will receive outpatient treatment or be hospitalized. If you're hospitalized and stay in the emergency ward until midnight, this amount covers your hospitalization, excluding medication costs. If you are hospitalized, the cost per night is a few liras, and you can use insurance for this." She explained everything to me in detail. I accepted and paid the 600 liras. The doctor who came for examination also explained the treatment process: "I will order a test for you to determine if it's a virus or bacteria. If it's a virus, your treatment process will be as follows, and if it's bacteria, the treatment process will be different." My illness was viral, and I was hospitalized in the emergency ward. It was decided that I would take another test, and if it came back normal, I would be discharged. Another nurse who came to administer the injection also explained all the steps of receiving and administering the medication, potential side effects, and the remaining treatment process to me calmly and thoroughly. In fact, from the moment of arrival to departure, the visitor became familiar with the entire process.

Inspired by the flexible rules of this hospital, I also defined the "Acibadem" law for my company, requiring myself and my employees to fully explain the buying and selling process to the customer. This means that when someone wants to buy or sell a car from our dealership, we explain the entire process from start to finish to the customer.

In my opinion, when a customer is dissatisfied with our services, we must pay whatever they demand to satisfy them. When they are satisfied and receive double their losses, in the next stage, we also send a bouquet of flowers to their home and then invite them and their family as guests of AutoShenas to a famous restaurant in the city.

The "Two Free Gifts" Plan

In this plan, the customer is asked to provide all their and their family's details and biography in a form tailored to their preferences. Two free gifts are offered by AutoShenas to the customer, who specifies to whom they will present these two gifts.

When they come to pick up their car, a suitable gift for the age and taste of one of their family members is placed on the car dashboard as a gift. Their favorite perfume is also placed in the car. These gestures are extended to a wider range of connections, and even two gifts are sent by AutoShenas to the persons referred by the customer.

In my opinion, this method is the best form of advertising for attracting future customers and ensuring the satisfaction and peace of mind of our previous customers. Many staff members question me, saying, "Mr. Khosravani, how profitable is it to provide free gifts and services to customers instead of just changing the oil for them?" In response, I say, "If you were as trusted as I am and knew that these types of advertisements make our company unique and keep us at the forefront, today you would be sitting in this management chair instead of me."

Types of Guarantees

At AutoShenas and Auto Khosravani, we offer three types of guarantees:

1- One-week Return Guarantee: A car purchased from us comes with a one-week guarantee along with the car's registration. If within a week the car's condition is different from what is stated in the registration, the customer can return the car, and we also impose a five percent penalty on ourselves. I have considered this five percent penalty as a punishment for ourselves so that we do not make such mistakes again.

2- Replacement Guarantee: If the engine or gearbox of the car develops a fault within a year, the defective car is taken back, and another brand-new car is given to the customer without any extra charge.

3- One-year Engine and Gearbox Guarantee: This guarantee is for second-hand cars. We guarantee the engine and gearbox for one year, during which the customer can visit AutoShenas for free repairs. This is conditional on the buyer visiting AutoShenas every 5000 kilometers and using the car warranty card.

AutoShenas Emergency Card

This emergency card is not just for breakdowns. Sometimes, the driver may not be able to drive due to illness or fatigue. In such situations, they can contact our car emergency service, and by sending a driver on our behalf, both the car and the driver reach their destination safely.

I hope that before I leave this world, I can bring AutoShenas to the ideal and international standard level that I aspire to.

For individuals entering our organization for work, if they do not have financial ability to purchase a car, they can work for us by paying a percentage to the company, and if they do not have financial ability to purchase a car, we will procure a car for them.

For example, a mechanic who wants to work for us can earn a fixed salary and a percentage of the contract. In a situation where a young person comes to us looking for work and, as they say, has no work experience or no financial stability, if they are willing to work and are committed and responsible, after completing the necessary training courses can also be recruited into our organization.

Over the past two years, we have concluded that if we want to expand AutoShenas, we must first strengthen it and properly address the flaws in the organization.

At present, AutoShenas has become profitable and has almost become a famous brand in its field. It has found its place in the market, and its infrastructure is ready. With small and incremental steps, we are expanding AutoShenas.

We train young people quickly and then expect them to serve in AutoShenas under our working conditions.

We also employ female mechanics here, and working conditions are easily available for all segments of society.

In my opinion, the best way to make money in Iran is providing good service to customers. Good service, along with respect, attracts many customers to your business and ensures that people line up to give money and receive services from such a company, and they welcome it well.

We lack respect in our society. For example, you can observe in these tough economic conditions the public's preference for a particular restaurant in the city, which enjoys higher income compared to other restaurants. The sole reason for this profitability lies in the level of respect and service provided by the restaurant's staff to its customers, not just the quality and delicious taste of the food.

In my personal life, I also adhere to this approach, finding pleasure in the act of purchasing, even if the item's price is several times higher than its original value. In essence, I value the experience of buying and genuinely enjoy it.

Most of the time, some people criticize me, alleging that I favor the affluent and wealthy, serving only the top four percent of wealthy people in country. In response, I clarify that I've tailored these conditions for affluent mindsets, not just affluent individuals.

For instance, when entering a gas station, one may notice a variety of cars. It's possible to observe that sometimes, the generosity of a driver with a more economical car model towards a gas station attendant surpasses that of a BMW owner. Essentially, the driver with the more economical car possesses a wealthy mindset, rather than the BMW owner. I engage with people who shows wealth and generosity of spirit.

Prospective individuals seeking to represent our dealership must align with and resonate with my affluent mindset.

AutoShenas Culture

As an employer, it's essential to treat respectfully with the customer. Customers should be greeted with a positive atmosphere upon entering AutoShenas. They should feel the distinction.

Note: It's worth mentioning that in many parts of the world, customers are not treated with the same level of respect, and complimentary services are not commonly offered.

Today, I can confidently assert that AutoShenas surpasses many service centers worldwide. While others excel in one or two areas individually, we have managed to excel and thrive in all aspects within our organization. Nevertheless, I acknowledge that modern countries boast stronger organizational structures than ours, and their emphasis on robust and cohesive organization is unmistakable.

AutoShenas Challenges

During the first year, we didn't have many customers, and as a result, few service personnel remained in this profession. Additionally, when customers arrived, I didn't have access to professional and experienced staff. I encountered various difficulties in this regard but ultimately managed to strike a balance by establishing respect with customers, earning their trust.

Business in the Iranian Market

Years ago, while teaching in "Blue Ocean" classes of Dr. Sehhat, I encountered students, mostly PHD graduates in marketing from foreign universities, who attended these educational classes to learn about trading in the Iranian market. I always told them: "Trading in the Iranian market has its own nuances and rules. For instance, while silver might be the best-selling color globally, it's not necessarily the case in Iran. Another example is traditional saffron-flavored ice cream or its cone, recognized as a symbol of ice cream in Iran."

In the automotive sector, contrary to other countries worldwide, in the Iranian car market:

People's top priority is affordability, with quality ranking fourth. (Our artificial intelligence unit has proven this after six months of research.) For example, when choosing between an American and a Korean car, customers prefer the Korean one because Korean cars depreciate less in Iran than American ones.

The second priority is the availability of spare parts, not price.

The third priority is brand and options. (However, there is very little difference between the second and third priorities.)

Quality is the fourth priority.

Therefore, if you intend to launch a car in Iran:

First: You must establish a market for second-hand cars.

Second: Advertise the availability of the desired car's spare parts across Iran.

You must be able to market every type of car and type of customers. You need to recognize the attractions of each customer. Your desired car should be the customer's top choice. Find the product's position and then start your advertising in that position. To advertise and introduce a new car to the market, first promote its parts under the desired brand name and let the car's name, along with its parts, take root in people's minds and memories.

In my opinion, the Iranian market is very similar to the Indian market. In India, people sell their house to buy tickets to go to the cinema and watch the lives of Bollywood stars. Similarly, in Iran, ordinary people are very inclined to follow the lifestyle of affluent and wealthy individuals. That's why certain bloggers in Iran have more followers and fans than global standards. It's crucial to understand that for product offerings in Iran, having knowledge and quality isn't necessarily as important and effective; you must understand the twists and turns of the Iranian market. To reach this level, you must start by apprenticing. This approach applies worldwide. For instance, to open a McDonald's branch, it's necessary to apprentice at McDonald's for two to three years.

The Best Businesses in Iran

First Priority: Continuing the family business, provided you're interested. If you follow in your father's footsteps and expand that profession and trade, you're starting your work from a higher point than zero. You've learned the ins and outs. You have a lot of experience and start the job from a higher step than others. Second Priority: Pursue a career that you're passionate about.

You must start apprenticing in your desired field from the zero point, even if you have initial capital to start the business. Invest that cash capital wisely and start apprenticing empty-handed. Because Rome wasn't built in a day. Sufficient experience doesn't come overnight or with having a lot of capital. Experience only comes from working and overcoming all the hardships. The advantage of this method is that if you realize halfway that you're not interested in this job or you can't do it, you haven't suffered much during the apprenticeship and you can start again from the start point.

Final Recommendation

To the youth, enthusiasts, and everyone reading this book, I recommend:
- First and foremost, be passionate about your lifestyle and work.
- Don't overlook presenting creative ideas and don't be afraid of the gap between reality and your dreams.
- Have the courage to dream.
- Challenge existing beliefs and always strive to set your goals a little higher with every step you take. Doing so allows you to go beyond any limitations.
- Just dreaming won't achieve any goals. That's why see the difficulties of your life as important opportunities that accelerate your growth.
- Always remind yourself that everything that happens to you ultimately benefits you. If you always seek the lessons that life

gives you, you will ultimately become stronger, wiser, and better.

• And always remember that the strongest personalities are imbued with the deepest wounds.

Analysis of the Success Factors of
AutoKhosravani and AutoShenas

Why are some people more successful than others? This simple question is exactly what has led to the development of success literature and success knowledge. In fact, if we consider the thinking process, as Anthony Robbins says, as a process of asking and answering questions, it is through asking questions that knowledge is formed. So, if you want to gain knowledge in the field of success, you need to start with questions like:

- Why do some people become more successful?
- Why do some people act more successfully?
- Why do some people fail to achieve their goals despite their efforts?
- What are the most important variables related to success?
- What role do each of these variables play in this process and what weight and significance do they have?

These questions help your mind focus on finding answers,

which can guide you towards success. Understanding these answers and discussing them can show you clear paths to follow. Knowledge is all about behaviors and information that lead to repeating certain outcomes. Knowing how to succeed is crucial. It helps you adopt the right strategies and keep going. Most failures happen because of wrong strategies. Learning from success stories can help us find the best strategies. For instance, imagine you need to stay focused on your tasks. You learn from someone like Remi Garde, who climbed seven high peaks on seven continents. He says: "Focus on your goal and keep moving forward. Do things you can control and don't let doubt distract you. Doubt and focus don't mix. Clear your mind of doubts to stay 100% focused. Don't worry about failing; just focus on your goal! Fear, worry, or stress can make us doubt ourselves. Learn to control fear, worry less, and manage stress. These are all mental processes. Sometimes, having a mindset of 'whatever happens, happens' can help a lot (that's what I did when I first jumped with a parachute!)."

In such books, you'll learn that getting rid of doubt and hesitation is crucial for success because they're major distractions. Success requires focus and determination, so it's important to eliminate doubt. Here, you leave behind indecision and uncertainty, realizing that doubt is more destructive than making mistakes. This small piece of knowledge helps you act against doubt and hesitation, which you might not have done otherwise. But where does success knowledge come from? It comes from curious minds and individuals who've tried to follow a path to success. These individuals have gathered their knowledge and experiences, leaving them as lessons and legacies. Altogether, this helps us understand what's right and what's wrong. This collection forms the literature of success. In recent decades, the publication of successful people's life stories has enriched this literature even more. This is happening today with the publication of Ali Khosravani's biography, a reputable figure in the Iranian car trading industry. This book can convey valuable insights to those interested in working in the car industry."

Ali Khosravani's biography, a reputable figure in the Iranian car trading industry, is another example of such books; a book that can convey abundant insights to individuals interested in working in the automotive sector.

Chapter One

There's a common misconception in the realm of success, and indeed in society, that suggests if someone emerges from affluent families with ample resources, they won't be particularly successful or will be viewed as less successful. Many believe that to achieve success, one must start from scratch or even below scratch and work their way up to a self-made success story. However, this notion is entirely misguided and incorrect.

The Root of the Problem

The reason behind such misguided clichés is our lack of a proper understanding of success. Success means having a goal and moving from your current position towards your desired destination. Now, everyone's goal can be unique, and the path can vary accordingly, depending on this goal. Therefore, your starting point might be ahead of others, and consequently, your desired destination could also be further ahead. Hence, clichés like "you won't be successful if you come from a wealthy family" should be discarded because they lack any basis in logic or reason.

For success, it's essential to make the most of all available opportunities around us. Why subject ourselves to unnecessary hardships and venture to distant places if there are opportunities and possibilities nearby? There's a book called "The Seekers of Gurdjieff" which sheds light on this matter. Gurdjieff was a renowned contemporary Sufi master who drew inspiration from various Middle Eastern Muslim scholars. Gurdjieff, of course, had his own disciples. One of his disciples, who was European, became fascinated with finding his master's mentors. This led him on extensive journeys to the Middle East, India, Central Asia, and beyond.

A fascinating aspect of this individual's story was that after months and years of searching, he realized that finding Gurdjieff's mentors wouldn't alleviate his inner struggle. If he believed that Gurdjieff himself was crucial, then he needed to seek the teachings and principles that shaped such a personality. Eventually, he transformed into a seeker himself and discovered that near his own place of residence, there existed a center where he could attain the authentic teachings and guidance he sought.

This rule of "what you seek is already within you" appears in various other books as well. Interestingly, many individuals during their youth and adolescence believe that what they possess in their surroundings isn't suitable for them. However, it's astonishing to realize later in life that they wish they had paid attention to these matters from their youth. Sometimes, opportunities are right within our reach, and it's illogical to overlook them due to societal misconceptions.

Living Among Cars

Ali Khosravani was born and raised in a family where his father was involved in construction work and car trading. He grew up in an environment filled with cars and their hustle and bustle, as he himself described it. Well, what's wrong with growing up in such an environment and pursuing such a career? He could have certainly ventured into other fields and occupations, and his father would have allowed him to do so. But when such opportunities exist around someone, why should they abandon them and pursue other ideas and businesses?

A significant part of success lies in recognizing opportunities and responding positively to them, whether it means embarking on long journeys to discover them or simply looking around oneself.

Chapter Two

Where do you stand in your business field? If you're not first, then perhaps it doesn't matter much if you're second, eighth, or eighteenth. The crucial thing is not being first. In branding, it's often said that you remember the firsts and the biggest in a field. For instance, do you remember who was the second person to climb Mount Everest? But you most likely remember the first. Those who come second or later often fade from memory, even if their situation is quite good. It's the same in business; you must strive to be the first and the foremost brand. The key point here is that perhaps you won't be first, and you might not even become first, but your mindset, spirit, and drive should be aimed at being first and becoming the top brand. It's about having that drive towards being the first and having others remember your name first in your business. In that case, you'll need minimal advertising and marketing because everyone will remember you and introduce you to others.

Why Aim for First Place?

But why aim to be first in your business? What if you're not first? The main point is not just about being first and reaching the summit but having the mindset to strive towards being first. In fact, the main goal is to be prepared for being first and to undergo the necessary training, not just to go and reach it. Because we all know that sometimes we can be first in a field and sometimes we can't. It's not because of our weakness that we sometimes can't, but rather because of the strong position of others. This needs to be deeply understood. The important point is that our minds should be filled with the idea and belief that we must be first. This idea and belief drive us to create specific values, goals, and daily rhythms, which is a very important point in these daily routines.

Darren Hardy's Insights

In his book "The Compound Effect," Darren Hardy offers intriguing insights into success through checklists published at the end of the book. In the checklists related to values, he points out that:

A checklist of one's values throughout life functions like a GPS, determining its direction and obstacles along the way. Here, we present a checklist that can confront you with your real values:

- Who in your life holds significant importance to you, and what values in this person have led to this significance for you?
- Who are my best friends throughout my life, and what qualities do they possess?
- If I had the magical power to acquire a specific trait, and this trait was given to me, which one would I prefer?
- What are three of my biggest dislikes throughout life?
- Which three individuals in the world do I dislike the most, and why?

In the realm of checklists, it is noted that sometimes aversion to being second or losing, etc., can be one of your most constructive values. Why not? It's not just love and affection that can propel you forward; sometimes your dislikes and aversions can also determine your direction, just like a GPS, providing the background, timing, and direction of your movements.

After the checklist of values, we move on to the checklist of habits. Darren Hardy writes about this:

We've talked about the power of habits and the significant positive and negative impacts they can have on our lives in a section of "The Compound Effect". But the next crucial point is to make sure we arm ourselves with the habits needed for the goals and values we've set. This checklist helps you delve deeper into this point.

- What goals do I have?
- What habits need to be ingrained within me and added to my personality to achieve these goals?
- For example, to achieve a specific income over the course of a year, what habits do I need?
- Am I an early riser?
- Do I dedicate an hour daily to productive and positive reading?
- Am I a team player?
- Do I utilize creativity and innovation in my work?
- Do I add ten to twenty new clients to my business weekly?
- Am I proactive in addressing the concerns of my dissatisfied customers?
- Do I have good speed of action?
- Have I created a considerable relative advantage for myself?
- And...

Remember, at this stage, you should also pay attention to your negative habits; habits that need to be eliminated along this path. These habits should become a rhythm throughout the days that can lead you to your goal.

Routines Aimed at Being the Best

This is where we delve into the most critical aspect of success: establishing daily routines geared towards our chosen goal. Our objective is to excel and lead in our respective fields. Therefore, it's only natural that we adopt habits that align with this ambition. These habits may involve increased practice, study, networking, time management, sales efforts, and more. Essentially, anything that moves us forward from our current position. These daily routines and habits, focused on achieving the top spot, are our most valuable assets in business. The key isn't just reaching the goal; it's about consistently striving to be the best and surpassing our previous selves each day. If we adhere to these routines diligently, we won't tire of our successes, both big and small, and we'll keep progressing. Essentially, our minds should be filled with the belief, dream, and goal that our primary mission in business is to succeed. Winning may mean different things to different people, depending on their goals and relative advantages. Therefore, the paths to preparing for this success and being at the forefront can vary greatly. The crucial point here is to cultivate readiness for such a state within ourselves.

Chapter Three

You're probably familiar with Tai Lopez, one of the world's top marketers and salesmen who has managed to monetize himself to the tune of hundreds of millions of dollars. In one of his clips, he talks about sales and marketing, and his insights are quite intriguing. Let's review some of his remarks in a list-like format to get to the main point:

Every business comprises three main components: products and services, resources and facilities, and finally, sales and marketing.

At the beginning of my career, I spread my focus evenly across all three components. I neglected the Pareto principle. However, later on, I realized that eighty percent of your time, money, energy, and education should be devoted to marketing. Without marketing, you don't have money, and without money, you don't have customers.

You need to create the best mousetrap. The world won't beat a path to your door if they don't know about it. In that case, your products and services will be useless.

Your product isn't the centerpiece; marketing is. All your money comes from people. So, you need to understand that your products and services relate to people.

Why do we shy away from sales and marketing? Because we're not good at it. It's natural to distance ourselves from things we're not good at.

Sales is one-dimensional, while marketing is multi-dimensional. There are hundreds of ways to market; email, blogs, teleseminars, and so on. You don't even need to speak face to face with someone.

Marketing should be done in a way that resonates with you and brings you joy. I market in a teaching style; speaking, motivating, and teaching. I teach and speak and ultimately invite people to my products.

I used to hate sales because I had a bad experience with it. I detested one-on-one sales. Insults, humiliation, contacting the police, and even sending dogs were experiences I had from one-on-one sales in homes. These experiences gradually made me feel worthless, while there were pleasant ways to market, and I wasn't aware of them.

Everything in life is about energy and movement. If you genuinely enjoy marketing, others will notice your passion. However, if you approach marketing half-heartedly, your lack of energy and effectiveness will be evident.

Let go of the term "selling." Instead, focus on solving someone else's problem and getting compensated for it. Think of yourself as a consultant rather than a salesperson. Use the word "help" instead of "sell."

I enable people to understand that I can assist them. This approach helps me avoid feeling rejected.

Every successful marketing campaign begins with crafting compelling content. Write in a way that makes people feel they need your product or service immediately. Sadly, 99% of businesses overlook this. My advertisements must lead directly to swift purchases.

People often believe in making modest promises and exceeding them. However, I advocate for making bold promises and surpassing them by a significant margin. Why not do both? Make a grand pledge and deliver even greater results. If you only offer modest promises, it becomes uninspiring, and people lose interest.

People typically have two key questions. If you can address these inquiries effectively, they'll gravitate towards you: Why should I make a purchase? Why should I choose you? Remember, people make emotional purchases and then justify them logically.

The strange tale of sells

Sales, in fact, tells a curious tale that dominates both the beginning and end of our modern world. In truth, we all, in some capacity, engage in sales, and no one can deny their connection to it. A teacher sells their educational services, a shopkeeper sells their products, an engineer sells their expertise, a doctor sells their medical knowledge, and so forth. Hence, understanding sales and mastering the art of selling should be considered essential knowledge and skills that everyone should possess, learn, and utilize to the fullest. However, many harbor an aversion to sales, often equating it solely with being a door-to-door salesperson. Yet, as Tai Lopez asserts, we must grasp those sales extends far beyond mere face-to-face interactions. At times, sales evolve into broader endeavors such as marketing, and it's crucial to recognize that it can encompass various approaches and strategies.

From Sales to Consultancy

The first crucial aspect of sales is consultancy. Indeed, the initial change that triggers subsequent transformations in salespeople is understanding that their job isn't merely about selling; as Brian Tracy puts it, their job is to provide consultancy to others. Brian suggests that wherever he went to provide consultancy, he would ask salespeople, whom he was supposed to train, not to identify themselves as salespeople but as consultants who aim to guide individuals in their field of expertise, even writing "consultant" on their business cards. This shift in terminology led to a change in belief, which, in turn, prompted behavioral changes. This shift in behavior, in turn, led to others treating them kindly, while also improving their own sense of well-being. Ultimately, it's crucial for an individual to view themselves as a consultant rather than just a salesperson; naturally, being a consultant fosters a better sense of purpose. A consultant is driven to exert more effort in conveying better information to others, and this structural change results in improved performance.

The Man Who Loved Sales

When we examine the life of Ali Khosravani, we observe a strong emphasis on being a salesperson. For the largest private car salesperson in Iran, matters such as the brand, performance, type, factory, and manufacturing company of cars are not as important as the sales process itself. In essence, he enjoys persuading and advising others, establishing relationships with them, and ultimately succeeding in selling them a car. It's this process that matters most to him, which is why he has been so successful in his career.

Once, Hitchcock travels to France. The airport official checks his visa and sees that it says "producer." Hitchcock, in fact, is one of the greatest horror filmmakers in the world, and one of the most significant figures in cinema history. The airport official asks him, "What do you produce?" Hitchcock replies, "I produce fear." Similarly, it seems that this is the case for Ali Khosravani: he is actually in the process of producing sales techniques and creativity in that field. Perhaps it would be better to call him a producer of car sales methods, rather than just a car salesperson.

The Sales Specialist

Khosravani enjoys providing guidance to others and offering valuable insights about cars, enabling his customers to make purchases confidently. Many of us have likely experienced frustrations with unprofessional behavior and disorganized sales tactics from salespeople or companies when shopping for goods and services. It's akin to visiting a store and being hounded by salespeople in a disrespectful manner to explain the prices of various items like shoes, clothes, and so on. Ali Khosravani recognized these issues and, as a result, sought to revolutionize sales techniques. He aimed to become a pioneer in developing new and improved methods for selling cars, ensuring that customers could trust him implicitly and be fully satisfied with their purchases. From his communication style to negotiating with customers and imparting information, Khosravani focused on excelling in every aspect. He provided top-notch training to his team so that they could deliver the best buying experiences. Consequently, he effortlessly rose to prominence and became the best in his field. Essentially, we encounter someone who is an expert in sales rather than just a car enthusiast, and this distinction is pivotal in understanding his biography.

Chapter Four
Ethics of Work

The ethics of work often go unnoticed, yet they hold immense importance. But what exactly do we mean by the ethics of work? It means valuing work for its intrinsic worth, rather than solely for the social recognition it may bring. Many people gauge the significance of their work based on societal perceptions, believing that their work must be grand or unique to matter. However, true significance lies in the act of working itself, not in the scale or novelty of the work. There's a famous saying attributed to a Christian priest that underscores this idea: the importance of work lies in the love with which it is done, not in its grandeur or scale. Similarly, in discussions about work ethics, the focus is on the value of work for the act of working itself. Work helps us distance ourselves from conditions like poverty, depression, and illness, enabling us to positively impact society and serve others.

Working is a goal itself

Kim Woo Chung, in his book "Every Street Is Paved with Gold," sheds light on a prevalent attitude among Korean youth in the 1990s who viewed work merely as a means to attain a comfortable life. He considers this mindset a grave insult to work ethics and regards working itself as a noble and sacred goal. Working allows us to serve our communities and fellow human beings. If you can adopt such a perspective, work becomes a source of complete happiness. You don't work because it might lead to your happiness; you work because happiness lies in working itself. With this mindset, you can even find fulfillment in the smallest and seemingly insignificant tasks, and accumulating these qualities can ultimately lead to remarkable success.

Points about Mr. Sohrab

One of the fascinating aspects of Ali Khosravani's life is his father's approach, whom he referred to as Mr. Sohrab. Although Ali was diligent in his studies, there came a time when his father intervened. His father went to the school and made significant efforts to hinder Ali's academic progress. Even when the school supervisor and principal insisted against such actions, his father called Ali and had a conversation with him. He told Ali that he had never compelled him to study, as a father should, but if he wanted to study, there was no obstacle, and if he didn't want to, there was still no obstacle. He wanted his son to clarify his duty and pursue it wholeheartedly, to start a task earnestly and see it through to the end.

Ali Khosravani's father always advised him, "Whatever you do, do it to the best of your ability. Even if you become an ordinary employee in an office, work so well and honorably that when they want to downsize, you'll be the last option for the office." This mindset was instilled in Ali and prompted him to approach every task with seriousness and strive to excel. We recognize this mindset as work ethics. In the words of Dr. Stephen Covey, in his book "The 7 Habits of Highly Effective People," which is among the most famous self-development books globally, you have two ways to build immense self-esteem: Set a goal and work towards achieving it.

Make commitments and promises to yourself and consistently adhere to them, always follow through with your actions.

In both cases, high self-esteem is cultivated within you. Self-esteem is not necessarily linked to external successes and will always remain within you. Embracing and adhering to work ethics and seriousness in work will foster such self-esteem within you.

Chapter Five

Today's world is characterized by its rapid pace, which influences the urgency in everything we do. From opting for fast food for meals to resorting to instant pills for weight loss or gain, and even seeking the fastest modes of transportation like cars, trains, and planes to reach our destinations swiftly, the desire for instant gratification pervades many aspects of our lives. Consequently, there's a significant allure towards quick success, with many individuals capitalizing on this trend to promote rapid pathways to success.

However, the reality is that true success doesn't come instantly. Darren Hardy, in his book "The Compound Effect," emphasizes this point early on, highlighting that there's no such thing as instant success. He asserts that success requires dedication and a significant investment of time, dispelling the notion of quick fixes. Arnold Schwarzenegger famously stated that success is built on repetition and consistent effort, without shortcuts. Success, therefore, is a gradual process, where each step forward brings new knowledge and strength. As Mas Oyama, the renowned martial artist, noted, overcoming each obstacle provides greater resilience and power for tackling the next challenge.

Understanding this process is essential. Success doesn't manifest suddenly; it requires sustained effort and perseverance. While the journey may present challenges akin to bitter stems, the fruits of success are sweet. Recognizing this, we must commit ourselves to the journey, embracing the gradual progression towards our goals with determination and resilience.

Progress in Process

Many experts attribute the slow progress of Iranians to a lack of thinking in steps. When asked to plan for ten, twenty, or even five years, many of us feel overwhelmed. We struggle to grasp what lies ahead in such long stretches of time. However, as time passes, we forget that success comes from taking small steps forward.

Those who don't approach success step by step, as Ali Khosravani's father suggests, often face quick setbacks. In the world of success, it's not just about making the first million or becoming a billionaire; it's about developing the right mindset along the way. When you focus on building that mindset, your success becomes lasting and steady.

A Brilliant Insight

Farzad Habibollahi, the football analyst for Persepolis team, shared some thoughts on Branko Ivanković's coaching philosophy before the start of the seventeenth league week. He believes this philosophy will be the key to Persepolis' success.

Consistency in success and maintaining sustainable achievements are crucial elements of personal growth. Many individuals achieve success, big or small, but without an understanding of how to sustain it, they often lose sight of future progress and accomplishments. This is where the idea of being process-oriented and progressively moving towards success becomes extremely important. Let's quote some of Farzad Habibollahi's insights on this topic. He served as the analyst for Persepolis during a period when the team, under Branko Ivanković's coaching, achieved remarkable results despite not having exceptionally talented players. However, what was the secret behind their consecutive championships, and why did their success seem perpetual? He writes:

The night before the game against Al-Rayyan in Tehran, I discussed football philosophy with Branko after dinner. The question was: 'Isn't one of the trickiest parts of a coach's job to harmonize inherently contradictory elements?' In your football philosophy, both players' patience during the game and their speed with the ball are necessary. 'Patience and speed.' Or: How can a coach remain relatively calm in various situations, yet keep his team hungry and aggressive? 'Calmness and maintaining an aggressive style of play.' Branko responded: 'I've always aimed to lead a normal life. Striving for normalcy and behaving normally has always been one of my lifelong goals. And what I want to instill in my team is the ambition to remain hardworking, yet relatively normal.' Two nights before the game against Al-Wahda in Tehran, when our victory alone wasn't enough, and we needed Al-Rayyan to draw with Al-Hilal in Qatar for Persepolis to advance from the group stage, Branko, at the dinner table with his assistants, talked about our inner desire to see our families happy after each victory. 'How fulfilling it is to win in football and see your family members proud of you. But this primary goal shouldn't be our focus. The primary goal is to remain hardworking. Hard work, if used as a means, can bring temporary success, but hard work should be the coach's and the team's goal to increase the likelihood of repeating success.' An hour ago, our last practice for the first week of the league was over, while one of the hardest working men of the team was still the head coach. A day before the league starts, this thought process runs through my mind: 'Victory brings peace. Peace brings laziness. Laziness brings disorder. And disorder brings defeat.' Reflecting on this cycle doubles the importance of Branko's emphasis on hard work. Any potential complacency resulting from success must be counteracted by avoiding laziness. Every team that has sustained success has played such a fundamental role in its work philosophy. Persepolis, less than two months ago, concluded a superb season by winning the Premier League and advancing to the Champions League final eight. But each of us must understand that the goal is to remain hardworking at the level of last season, as if there had been no championship. The goal goes beyond victory or seeing loved ones happy. The goal is to remain hardworking; something that can keep the team away from self-deception, laziness, disorder, and the inevitability of defeat...

The Safe Path

It couldn't be explained better than this—a philosophy for achieving sustainable personal and even organizational success. When you gradually tread a path and achieve success, it fundamentally shapes a lasting character within you; thus, success can be relatively enduring for you. It's no wonder that Mr. Sohrab, the father of Ali Khosravani, had such a strong belief in hierarchical progression. According to Khosravani: "My father strongly believed in hierarchy. I remember when I wanted to seriously start working, he allowed me to collaborate from the lowest level. I started with janitorial work, then became a water carrier and a motorcycle courier, and after a few years, I moved up to become a student and an office manager. Because I was very passionate about this work, I endured all the hardships."

It's through such a style that developments and progress are formed sustainably and ingrained in individuals. In this case, even if success comes later, there's no need to worry; what matters is that we are moving in that direction, and if we do achieve it, our success will be more enduring.

Chapter Six
The Power of Perseverance

Steve Jobs once famously said that fifty percent of an entrepreneur's success is pure perseverance, with the rest being attributed to other factors contributing to success and personal development. This sheer perseverance is crucial and must be taken seriously because significant changes need to be made and routines need to be altered for operations to run smoothly. Every entrepreneur must endure periods of hard work, even if they aim to streamline processes so their company or business can function independently.

The Diligent Mindset

To achieve great success through hard work, one must embrace and justify the effort required. There's no way around it. An exemplary figure in this regard is Kim Woo Choong, the founder of the influential company Daewoo. In his book "Every Street Is Paved with Gold," he shares:

"I'm among the busiest individuals to have ever existed. I spend over 200 days a year on overseas trips, not to mention the additional domestic travels. My workload is so demanding that

I often forget family birthdays and sometimes even my own. Surprisingly, I don't mind. In fact, I find joy in this busy lifestyle. My schedule is so packed that I hardly recall vacations or leisure time with family. I thrive on the hustle of work, finding immense satisfaction in it. That's why I've never taken a day off. This might seem odd to others, leading them to label me as a workaholic or even insane.

I firmly believe that wholehearted dedication guarantees success in any field, eliminating the need for worry. A person who gives their all to their work will never face failure. This conviction often prompts the question: Do I truly enjoy life? Frankly, I find such inquiries amusing. Why should one seek leisure and relaxation when work itself offers equal, if not greater, fulfillment? These questions arise from individuals who haven't experienced the joy of a purposeful, busy life. Unfortunately, they haven't grasped the true essence of work, which explains their inquiries.

Chapter Seven
The Power of Hard Work

Work isn't just about making a living or personal growth; it's also about contributing to the well-being of society. But how do people see it? Many simply view work as a means to money and material gain, which I find to be a big insult to the ethics of work. If you hold your work in high esteem and take pride in your profession, you'll find great joy in life. This principle goes beyond just work; it applies to education too. Merely studying to get a degree and a job isn't enough. You need to be fully engaged in learning and acquiring knowledge, even to the point where others might call you eccentric or obsessed. Diligent individuals have a unique spark. Anyone who embraces hard work and effort gains an extra power and brilliance. It's sad to see students who only see studying as a chore, and even worse are those who struggle to study at all.

People often ask me about my hobbies, and I sometimes struggle to answer. Sure, I enjoy casual activities, but I wouldn't call myself a pro at anything besides work. I've never even played golf, a popular pastime among business folks. But what is a hobby anyway? If it's something that brings you joy and happiness, then my only hobby is work because that's what truly excites me.

Before starting Daewoo, I worked for a family-owned company, and I was all in. No time for leisure; I worked tirelessly. I never took a day off and was always proactive. I found immense satisfaction in my work, and I still do. The thrill of sealing a deal or negotiating is far more rewarding than any movie or game of golf.

We were young and driven to develop our company and our country. Our determination gave us confidence. We believed in hard work and sacrifice, and it paid off. I always say, while others worked from 9 to 5, the Daewoo team worked from 5 am to 9 pm, achieving in 22 years what others did in 44. Our dedication and seriousness set us apart. We worked twice as hard, and it showed in our progress.

Paths in the Business World

- When you step into the world of business, your role typically falls into one of four categories:
- Employee or Worker: You work for others and earn a wage.
- Entrepreneur: You have specialized skills and work for yourself, providing services to others.
- Business Owner: You own a business or factory, employing others to produce goods or services.
- Investor: You invest your capital in ventures to generate profits.

Most people aim for roles in the third or fourth category, either owning a business or making profitable investments. But why? Because they believe these roles offer significant rewards and financial gains. However, as a bodybuilding champion once noted, while everyone talks about lifting weights, the squat rack at the gym is often empty! Similarly, as Ronnie Coleman, a legendary bodybuilder with numerous titles, put it: "Everyone wants to be a bodybuilder, but nobody wants to lift heavy weights." Many aspire to achieve entrepreneurial success or wealth through investments but are reluctant to endure the challenges.

The Pitfall of a Fixed Income

There's an intriguing perspective on the allure and pitfalls of steady jobs and fixed incomes. The notion is that steady employment is one of three factors that contribute to addiction. Why is that? Well, a steady job means trading your time for a regular paycheck, creating a dependency over time. You become accustomed to the security of a stable income and structure your life around it. After years of this routine, you develop a mindset and lifestyle that rely heavily on this steady income, like clocking in and out each day. Your mind becomes conditioned to this pattern, hesitant to explore beyond the safety net, and you may only occasionally entertain thoughts of breaking free and pursuing other possibilities.

The Tough Phases of Independence

At the start, it's tough for people to fully own up to their actions, their outcomes, and their successes. Taking complete responsibility right off the bat is a real challenge. Initially, nobody wants to admit they're solely responsible for all their setbacks. Who'd want to entertain such a thought? If you admit to being the cause of all the tough situations in your life, it's going to weigh heavily on your conscience. You'll keep questioning yourself: If that's the case, why did I make these mistakes? If they were mistakes, why didn't I fix them? If I had the power to fix them, why didn't I take action, and why did I feel so powerless?

In his book "The Compound Effect," Darren Hardy talks about a section called "Keeping Score." He suggests picking an area where you want to grow or improve and then checking how you're doing in that area. He believes many folks lack an understanding of their status in different areas. For example, he shares his own story of working hard in his youth but getting a shock when his accountant told him he owed hundreds of thousands in taxes. Not only did he lack that much money, but he also had no clue where it came from or where it went. His experienced accountant kindly reassured him that he wasn't the first in such a situation and had seen many others clueless about their financial flow because they didn't track their spending.

Hardy then points out that when you start tracking your actions and behaviors in a specific area, you'll be shocked at first because you won't believe such events are happening. You'll be taken aback initially, but as you get used to it, you'll gradually reach the responsibility stage and realize you must accept it. Once you do, you'll realize you need to take action. Essentially, this awareness is the same power that brings responsibility to you.

Why Responsibility Is Tough?

Taking responsibility is hard because, at first, you're not used to seeing yourself as the cause of all failures and shortcomings. But once you accept that reality and realize you need to rely on yourself to fix things, you start to adjust. The pain of becoming independent is exactly why it's challenging. Initially, realizing you're on your own can be shocking for days, months, or even years. But as you come to terms with it and understand it's an undeniable reality, accepting it changes you.

Independence, as Ali Khosravani describes in his autobiography, feels like being a branch separated from the tree and feeling insecure. At first, humans feel intensely insecure. At this point, two things can happen: either they go back to their previous safe state, or they become stronger. Many prefer to return to safety rather than choose the path of becoming stronger.

Fundamentally, humans must understand that the world is an insecure place. However, this shouldn't lead to entirely negative thinking. They must realize that this insecure world is a harsh reality. Therefore, they must take responsibility for their mental, emotional, physical, and occupational security. It's for this reason that even the weakest animals usually exhibit a high degree of adaptability to their surroundings and are, as we say, sharp and agile. Every day they wake up, they're forced to fight for their safety, which makes them continually stronger.

Ali Khosravani's story of independence reflects this theme. He could have chosen to stay with his father, work, and have complete security. But he preferred to pursue his destiny and independence, defining and achieving security for himself in an insecure world. It was tough for him to pay installments, make sales, manage his office's necessities, and pay his employees' wages at the outset. However, none of these things killed him; and what doesn't kill you undoubtedly makes you stronger. It was precisely these moments of strength that eventually allowed him to achieve his independence and stand on his own two feet—the very place many aspire to be but only dream about instead of working towards it.

From Kindness to Toughness

As we delve into the final section, let's quickly touch on some key points that shouldn't go unmentioned. These insights could serve as valuable guidance, helping each of you chart a better course or avoid potential pitfalls.

In one of his plays, William Shakespeare has his characters utter an intriguing line: "For goodness, you must be a little cruel." Initially, this might seem puzzling, but upon reflection, its profound truth becomes apparent. The essence is that excessive kindness to your children could ultimately hinder their future. It's important to be somewhat strict with them so they understand that the world isn't always as gentle as their parents are, and that achieving success often requires effort. Some parents struggle to strike this balance, which is a significant flaw in their parenting approach.

When Ali Khosravani parted ways with his father, he still felt his support from a distance. His father wasn't accustomed to providing direct support to his children; instead, he offered it indirectly. For example, he would assure those in the car sales trade that if Ali owed them money, he would guarantee repayment. Or, when giving money to his children, he would require them to do something in return, even if it was just cleaning the car. These ethical and parenting practices ensured that his children were raised with firmness and that excessive kindness didn't spoil them.

Workplace Wellness

Success is typically linked to doing things correctly. However, there are times when you might be doing things right but not heading in the right direction. It's essential not only to execute tasks correctly but also to ensure they align with your intended goals. By doing so, you gradually build a positive reputation and thrive in your endeavors. Some may believe that in the competitive business world, cutting corners is acceptable, and paying attention to such details is unnecessary. However, considering the compound effect, investing time and effort into doing things right and doing them properly over a few years will lead to overall success. It's like constructing a sturdy skyscraper, layer by layer, with a solid foundation. Eventually, it becomes a towering structure that withstands the test of time. This was the essence of the advice Ali Khosravani received from his father: if you want your voice to be heard, your appearance must always be impeccable, as people won't take you seriously when you're not well-presented. Similarly, there's a saying attributed to Imam Ali, emphasizing the power held by those who deserve it.

Working with Scientific and Up-to-Date Methods

One of the key aspects of Ali Khosravani's business was focusing on rationality and contemporary knowledge. Rather than sticking to traditional methods in the car buying and selling industry, he opted for a modern approach. He realized that traditional car sellers often lacked proper training, relying solely on trial and error. Therefore, he invited experts in various fields such as negotiation, body language, sales techniques, etc., to train himself and his staff. He believed that such training could make his workforce unstoppable, professional, and up-to-date. For instance, he enrolled in personality development courses to learn how to interact effectively with car buyers. Imagine an organization where employees are well-versed in sales techniques, negotiation skills, body language, telephone etiquette, personality assessment, and psychology. When you encounter such trained professionals, you feel respected and valued, enhancing your overall experience. Unfortunately, in Iran, we often lack such respect and dignity towards customers, which is a consequence of not adopting scientific, modern, and up-to-date approaches.

Building a Strong Brand

One of the great American entrepreneurs once emphasized the power of having a well-known and respected name, suggesting that it can open more doors for you than even writing a hundred books. However, simply having a famous name isn't always enough. That's where branding comes in. It's essentially what people say about you when you're not around, or how they perceive the products and services you offer. Nowadays, people often invest in brands rather than just products or services. A brand communicates what a product or service represents and whether it's worth further exploration. It's essential to reach a point where your name inspires trust and confidence in your audience.

The foundation of a successful brand lies in the quality of the product or service you provide. Without a strong and reliable offering, you won't make a lasting impression. Therefore, it's crucial to prioritize delivering quality from the outset. Then, you must differentiate yourself in the market, ensuring that you stand out. As Seth Godin suggests, you must find your "purple cow" – your unique selling point that sets you apart from the competition. Once you've identified this, you can confidently move forward, knowing you'll capture attention and make a lasting impression.

Ali Khosravani echoed this sentiment, emphasizing the importance of each brand's unique identity. He recognized that creativity and innovation are key to long-term success. With this understanding, he set out to establish his brand in the car buying and selling market. His brand focused on trustworthiness, quality, and the well-being of customers and salespeople alike. Through this approach, he successfully established the Auto Khosravani brand in the country.

Surprising Customers

In business management, gathering feedback from customers comes in various forms. Sometimes, a customer regrets using your services or products, and they won't return. Other times, they might have a typical interaction, where if they find a similar option elsewhere, they'd switch without hesitation. However, the pinnacle is when you manage to surprise your customers, leaving them in disbelief at the level of service you provide. Not everyone achieves such interactions with customers, which is why those who do are few and highly successful. Ali Khosravani's biography illustrates this point. He recognized the main issue in Iranian business: the lack of kindness towards customers. He identified this significant gap and made efforts to bridge it. He understood how much customers complain about this and saw these complaints as an opportunity rather than a burden. He didn't shy away from customer complaints; instead, he turned them into opportunities for improvement and innovation. Therefore, it's no wonder that he turned such kindness to customers and prioritizing them into his signature move, his unique stamp. He understood that his product wasn't just about selling a car; after all, cars are produced elsewhere. He defined his product as a service called the "healthy car purchasing process," where establishing a strong connection with the customer became of utmost importance.

100% Responsibility

What percentage of responsibility do you think lies with us in any field? Different people might give different percentages, ranging from zero to seventy or eighty percent. Darren Hardy mentioned attending a seminar on family communication once. The speaker asked, "What percentage of responsibility do you think you have in your marital life?" Everyone had their own number in mind. But then, the speaker suddenly wrote on the whiteboard: 0 to 100; meaning that you are 100% responsible without expecting anything from others. It's with such a mindset that success becomes inevitable because your mind is filled with such an understanding. Ali Khosravani believes that in our organization, we should receive training in a way that if a customer doesn't make a purchase, we should take full responsibility ourselves, not blame the customer. We've been inadequate in providing such a sale. This is what they call the 100% responsibility rule without any expectation from the other party.

A Different Perspective

Having a different and constructive perspective in business and personal development is of great importance. Arnold Schwarzenegger once mentioned that he had a great fondness for the burning sensation caused by heavy weightlifting. But why? Was he crazy? He explained that he had trained his mind in such a way: the body stops growing at eighteen, and if you apply excessive pressure to it after that age, it burns. Therefore, you're forced to either back off or come back stronger. So, the burning sensation resulting from muscle strain means growth, and I love growth. He had trained his brain this way, and with every burn from heavy weights, he felt like he was in paradise, while others thought he was crazy!

In a part of his biography, Ali Khosravani mentions that his brother came to him and said he was unlucky because he had received a one billion Toman tax bill. When Ali asked about the reason, he realized that his brother had an income large enough that only the tax amounted to one billion Toman. He told his brother that he should actually be happy because he had earned so much that even if the tax bill were ten billion Tomans, he should be happy and overcome it. Essentially, billion-dollar taxes mean entry into the billionaires' club, and that's a congratulatory achievement! Yes, such a perspective on business essentially keeps a person from ever getting tired and sees every difficulty as an opportunity to move forward.

The End

Iranian Great Entrepreneur Books are originally created by *Great Entrepreneur Institution* in Iran and you can access their books in Iran through this here:

www.karafarinanebozorg.com

Also, to access books all around the world click bellow:

www.kidsocado.com/greatentrepreneur

How to access kidsocado Publishing House

www.kidsocado.com/shop

www.ingramcontent.com/pod-product-compliance
Lightning Source LLC
Chambersburg PA
CBHW052149070526
44585CB00017B/2037